Correction Officer's Guide to Understanding Inmates

The Forty-Four Keys to
Power, Control, and Respect

By:

LARONE KOONCE

Correction Officer, Ret.

Koonce Publishing First Edition 2012

Published in the USA by Koonce Publishing, Atlanta, GA.

ISBN: 978-0-9834837-0-0

Printed in the United States of America

To My Wife, Karen, and My Son, Andrew
L.K.

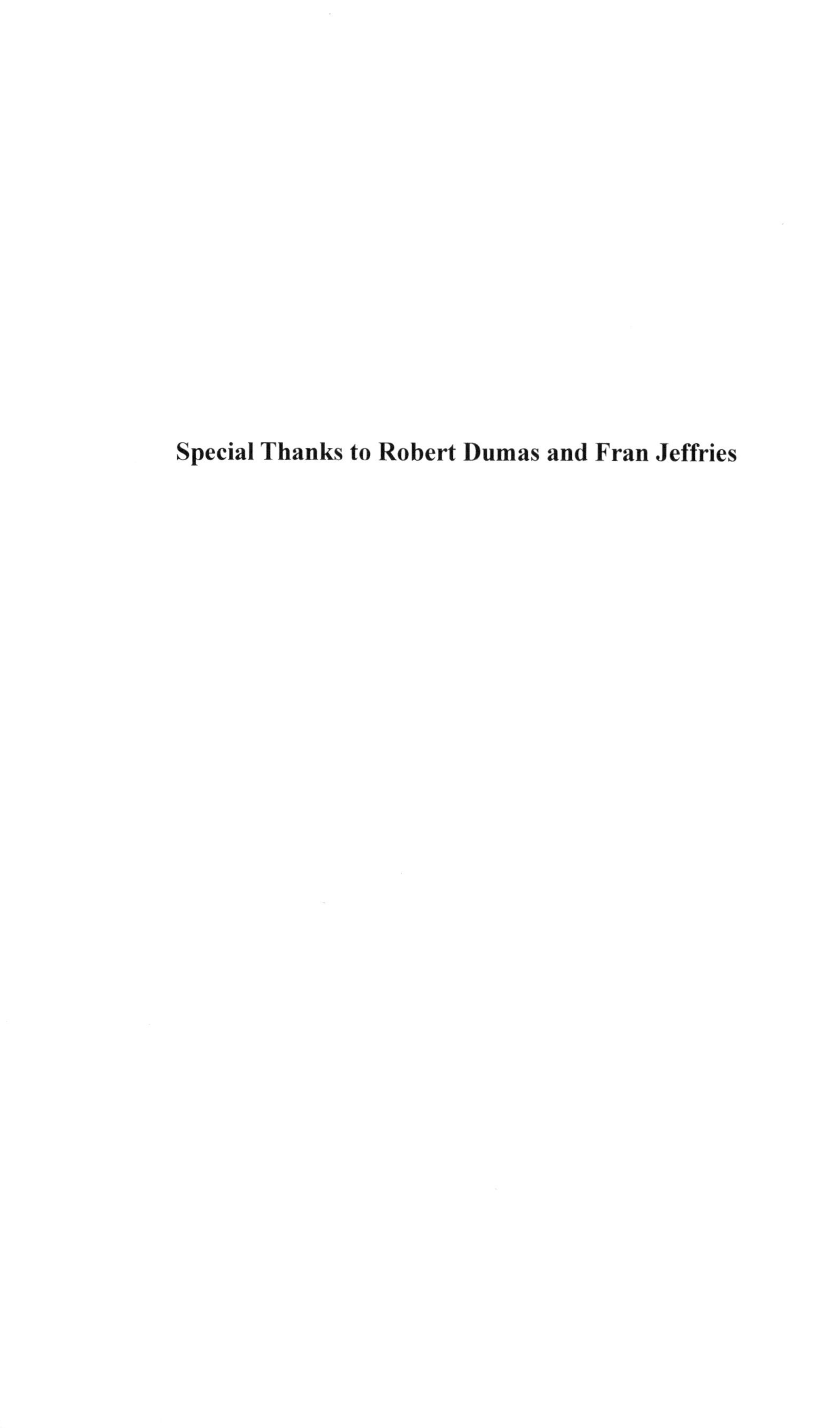

Special Thanks to Robert Dumas and Fran Jeffries

CONTENTS

INTRODUCTION

I became a New York City correction officer in 1987 at the age of twenty-two and retired in 2005 at the age of forty-one. I have no permanent scars or physical injuries, and I have no medical problems or conditions as a result of my service. I have not learned all the secrets of the universe, but there's one thing I do know and that's how to jail.

I, like most of you, did not have a relative or family friend in the department that pulled strings for me. I didn't have a hook. I couldn't make a phone call to get a steady post or to get a supervisor off my back. But throughout my career I was lucky enough to come across senior officers who took an interest in me and taught me what I needed to know to make the job work for me.

Now, I want to pass on what I have learned to you. Why take a career's worth of experience and put it on the shelf when I can share it with you? You shouldn't have to learn things the hard way, the way I and many other officers did. You shouldn't have to reinvent the wheel.

As I mentioned, I am retired. I receive a pension from the New York City Employees Retirement System (NYCERS) not the New York City Department of Correction. My pension is guaranteed to me until the day I die so, I am free to say whatever I want about the Department of Correction without having to worry about any negative ramifications. But I'm not writing this book to bash or embarrass the department, on the contrary, the department was good to me and in retrospect I can honestly say that I had a very good career. I have no axe to grind.

I have written this book to help officers who are trying to work their way through the maze that is the Department of Correction. I want to help those officers make it to retirement without being mentally or physically injured like so many of my friends and colleagues. I have seen officers lose their marriages, their families, their health, their jobs, and their lives during my years in corrections, and I want to prevent as many officers as I can from going down that path.

Who This Book Is For?

This book can help any officer at any stage of his career—thinking about becoming a correction officer, just starting the academy, or preparing for retirement. I want to help you stay safe, positive, healthy, and focused. I want to show you how to work the job and not let the job work you.

This book is for anyone who wants to know what it's like to be a correction officer. If you are thinking about becoming a correction officer or prison guard, this book will help you decide whether you have what it takes to work in a jail or a prison. In this book you will learn about the techniques and skills an officer must develop to effectively work with inmates and control their behavior.

If you are a correction officer or prison guard, you will find this book helpful. It will teach you how to gain the respect and confidence of the inmates, which is critical to your personal safety and getting the inmates to comply with your instructions. It also teaches you how to deal with those disruptive inmates who negatively influence other inmates. You will also learn how to form long-term working relationships with your fellow officers and supervisors.

Balancing your work life with your home life is critical to being an effective correction officer or prison guard. This book will help you maintain an even temperament and positive attitude at work and at home. The techniques discussed in this book will be helpful to any officer or prison guard, and if applied correctly, they will serve you well throughout your career.

This book is also for jail and prison supervisors. Although most supervisors started their careers in corrections as officers or guards, as they ascend through the ranks it is not uncommon to become disconnected from the issues and concerns of the rank and file, the front-line officers. This book will help supervisors reconnect with the issues and concerns of the officers they supervise and remind them of the challenges they faced when they were in the trenches.

This book is also for jail and prison administrators. Many officials and administrators of correction departments that are responsible for creating the guidelines and policies that govern the way a jail is run have never actually worked with inmates in a jail or prison. This book will help administrators understand the concerns and challenges that officers and prison guards face when carrying out these policies. One of the goals of this book is to give administrators insight into the challenges officers face and ultimately lead to better and more effective policy making.

Most importantly, this book is for the officer or prison guard who is disillusioned with the job and frustrated with dealing with hostile and unruly inmates and supervisors who just don't understand. For these officers this is the book you've been looking for. I, like you, was a disillusioned and frustrated officer who was beginning to doubt that corrections was right for me. I was able to turn my outlook around by learning from the senior officers the techniques needed to make being a correction officer or prison guard a rewarding experience. My hope is that this book will reboot your career, give you a fresh, new outlook on corrections, and help you achieve the respect you deserve from the inmates, your fellow officers and supervisors. This book will help you evolve into that effective, dedicated officer that you always knew you could be.

This Book has Three Major Themes

Theme One: The first theme of this book focuses on what it means to be a Correction Officer* and how we earn the respect and trust of the inmates we supervise. When the inmates respect and trust you they will be compelled to comply with your commands and instructions. If the inmates don't respect you, they won't listen to you and in some cases will do everything in their power to prevent you from maintaining control of your assigned area.

In order to get them to respect and trust you, first you must understand the inmates and learn what will and will not motivate them to comply with your orders. This book covers common problems officers face and gives the officer problem-solving techniques that will help alleviate these common problems. It also covers core subjects like fairness and how to confront and control rebellious inmates.

Theme Two: This theme covers officers' working relationships with their supervisors. Running a jail or prison is a team effort. It requires that officers and supervisors work together as a team to maintain the good order of the institu-

** In the New York City Department of Corrections we are called correction officers; in other jurisdictions those who work in jails and prisons are called guards. For the purposes of this book I will be using the title correction officer to refer to the jail and prison staff who work directly with the inmate population.*

tion. Sometimes officers as well as supervisors lose sight of that goal and become adversaries. This book offers skills that will enhance the working relationship between the officers and the supervisors, and help cultivate a healthy and productive working relationship.

Theme Three: This theme focuses on an officer's personal relationships outside the job, personal health, and wellbeing. To be consistent and even-tempered on the job, you must have a stable life outside the job. This book discusses how to create and maintain a balance between your job and your home life.

When I use the terms jail or jailing as a verb and not as a noun, I am referring to the skill set that is needed to cope from day to day in a correctional system, similar to how a basketball player refers to playing ball as balling or dancers refer to what they do as dancing. Jailing is what we do, and just like basketball and ballet, it requires a certain degree of skill and proficiency.

I also would like to make it clear that this book is not just about inmates and violence because being a correction officer is about much more than that. Being a good correction officer is more about you and your self-awareness than it is about inmates and violence. I hope that by reading this book you will become more self-aware and realize that you are in control of your own destiny.

This is an honest book with real accounts of actual events that have occurred during the course of my career. The names have been changed to protect the identities of those involved in the events and incidents.

I have chosen to use the masculine default to streamline the prose. This choice is not meant to overlook the many brave and courageous women who serve as corrections officers or to imply that only men are inmates.

Key 1

Know What It Means To Be A Correction Officer

And what is the job of a correction officer.

Most people's knowledge of jail comes from Hollywood movies and television shows. Old James Cagney movies or television shows that glamorize jail and the inmates are presumed to be accurate by those who do not have experience working in jails with inmates. The truth is jail is very different from the way it is depicted in movies and on television. Jail is not as chaotic as you might think. Contrary to what is seen in the movies and on television, officers are in control of the jails, not the inmates. Although officers are always outnumbered, sometimes more than sixty to one, we still maintain control of the jails. This is no accident. It takes skilled and dedicated correction officers to maintain control of a jail twenty-four hours a day 365 days a year.

This chapter provides the answers to two very basic questions: What does it mean to be a correction officer and what is the job of a correction officer? After answering these two questions, the important concept of inmate-officer communication is discussed. This chapter will help you understand what being a correction officer is all about and provides a foundation for the chapters to come.

What It Means to Be a Correction Officer

The first thing you need to know is that inmates see you as an officer—a C.O. or police. In their minds, for the most part, you are just like the cop that arrested them or any other law enforcement officer. They don't tend to make the distinction between police officers and correction officers the way we do. Many of them don't like cops so they don't like correction officers, either.

Yes, I know, you are nothing like the cops that patrol your neighborhood. You're cool; you don't have anything personally against inmates, and that's good. But remember, once you put on that uniform and step into that jail you are a correction officer 100 percent, and you are connected to every other law enforcement officer. That's how the inmates see you.

Being a correction officer means you are a peace officer. You are a law enforcement officer empowered by your state, city, county, or the federal government to enforce correction law. It's not personal; it's business, and at times, it's a dirty business. You will not be sitting on the sidelines while violence is happening around you. You will be actively trying to prevent violence from happening or assisting in terminating violence that has already begun.

You and your fellow officers are the law, the police of the jail, the line that cannot be crossed.

Don't delude yourself into thinking that being a correction officer is just a job and you only took the job to make money. There are plenty of other, safer ways to make money. Many of us became correction officers because it is a stable job that pays fairly well. However, early on we discover that the desire to have stable employment is not enough to sustain your interest in being a correction officer. What you may not have realized when you first decided to become a correction officer is that you possess a heightened desire to do what is right and to contribute to society in a positive way. These latent traits become more and more apparent as time goes by. Not everyone possesses the ability to be a correction officer.

If you are a correction officer or desire to be one, look deeply into your past, and you will find the roots of this desire. In my case, I discovered that my parent's beliefs about right and wrong, public service and personal responsibility prepared me for a career in corrections. Your personal views on the subject of right and wrong, and your character will be the determining factors that will lead you to and sustain you in the field of corrections.

No amount of money should convince you to remain a correction officer if your heart isn't in it. The inmates know the difference between an officer that believes in what he is doing and an officer who is just going through the motions in order to collect a check at the end of the week. If you don't believe in what you are doing, you run the risk of being corrupted by the jail environment. Jail becomes a very dangerous and stressful place for those who are just going through the motions.

Hopefully you have realized or will come to realize that you have chosen to become a correction officer because you believe in justice and are willing to stand for what you believe in. You serve the public good by maintaining the custody of society's criminal inmate population. By doing so you make it possible for your family and other law-abiding citizens to walk the streets and feel secure while they sleep at night. You are a responsible citizen who wants to make your community and the world a better place.

If you are already a correction officer, study the correction law, penal law, and rules and regulations, and understand the power that has been entrusted to you. It is important for you to understand who you have become and what you represent. The journey to being a successful correction officer begins and ends with self-awareness.

Most inmates, at the point in their lives that we encounter them, are just the opposite of what you are. You choose to honor your positive energy and inmates choose to honor their negative energy. You are trying to give back to society and as a result, make it better. Inmates want to take from society and feel that society owes them something. You set a positive example for your children and your community. Inmates set a negative example for your children and destroy your community. You like order, and they like chaos because with chaos, they can get away with more destructive behavior.

I don't want to make it sound like all inmates are bad because that would be generalizing and too simplistic. But what I am saying is that by becoming a correction officer, you have accepted a degree of responsibility for the betterment of society and the inmate, for the most part, has not. Now, there are many reasons why inmates behave the way they do and run afoul of the law. Many have been neglected as children, were abused, are homeless, or are addicted to drugs. Some have no support system, and you are the closest thing to family that they will have. So, during the time that the inmate is in your custody you should be an example of correctness and fairness in the hope that he or she will adopt some of your ideals and begin to see the benefit in honoring their positive energy.

What Is The Correction Officer's Job?

Answer: The Correction Officer's job is the Care, Custody, and Control of inmates.

Care means ensuring that the inmates receive the things that the law says they are supposed to receive like food, clothing, shelter, medical attention, etc.

Custody means keeping them in jail and preventing them from leaving until their time has been served.

Control means enforcing a code of conduct the inmates must live by while they are incarcerated.

Correction Officers serve as part of the criminal justice system. Some correction officers mistakenly believe that punishment is part of their job. It is not. The judge and jury punish criminals by sending them to jail. ***Jail is the punishment.*** Society has determined that jail, in and of itself, is a suitable punishment for committing a crime.

Incarceration is a very serious punishment. Incarceration destroys the human spirit and robs the inmate of the most precious commodity—time. So, whenever you begin to think that the inmates shouldn't have it so easy, remember, no amount of cigarettes or snacks can make up for the loss of time spent behind bars or the loss of liberty and freedom. You are not required to further punish the inmates that are in your custody for crimes they have committed on the outside. So, don't burden yourself with that responsibility.

Your Appearance Counts

To gain the respect of the inmates, you must carry yourself in a respectful manner. Part of your image as an officer includes your appearance. Maintaining a neat and professional appearance shows that you understand and respect yourself and your position.

Take pride in your appearance by purchasing a uniform that fits you. Do not purchase a uniform that is too big or too tight. Your uniform should fit comfortably. Make sure your shirt sleeves and jacket sleeves are not too long. If you can't find a shirt or jacket that fits you, then buy a bigger one and have a tailor make the necessary alterations.

It only costs a few dollars. Keep your shoes shined—not just in the academy but also throughout your entire career. When your uniform gets old and worn, throw it out and get a new one.

Some young officers believe that wearing a worn uniform makes them look more experienced and gives them more credibility with the inmates. This is not true. The inmates know if you are new and inexperienced no matter how worn your uniform is. Every officer is inexperienced when he first begins his career, and there is nothing wrong with that. The inmates will not treat you with respect just because you have a worn uniform. However, they will have more respect for you if your uniform is neat and clean. If you are an older, experienced officer, set a good example for the new officers by maintaining your appearance.

Communication with Inmates

There's one thing that all good correction officers have in common: they all are able to communicate well with the inmates.

The ability to communicate is very important in correction work. So, don't be afraid to communicate with the inmates.

Inmates are human, and some things are common to all human beings. I've learned that every human being wants to be heard. So, take the time to listen to what the inmates have to say. Even if you can't change an inmate's predicament or situation, he or she will respect the fact that you took the time to listen.

If you don't communicate with the inmates you will always be the last one to know what is going on in your assigned area. Inmates can give you information about themselves and the activities of the other inmates that will help you maintain control and prevent serious incidents from happening.

If you have an open line of communication with the inmates, most of them will come to you with their problems and afford you the opportunity to help settle their disputes instead of taking matters into their own hands. This will cut down on the amount of violence among the inmates and create a safer living environment for the inmates, as well as a safer working environment for you and your fellow officers.

Some officers have a policy of only speaking with inmates if it is absolutely necessary and keeping all interaction with inmates to a minimum. This may work for some officers, but most experienced officers agree that having an open line of communication with the inmates is a good thing.

Never Let an Inmate Monopolize Your Time

It is a good idea to maintain an open line of communication with the inmates, however you must also set limits. Do not spend too much time talking with one inmate while neglecting what the rest of the inmates are doing. You must circulate around your assigned area and make your presence felt; you can't do that if you are stuck talking to one or two inmates for your entire tour of duty.

Some inmates may just want to hold an innocent conversation with you, but some others may want to distract you from your duties. They may want to keep you away from a certain area because other inmates are doing something that they are not supposed to do. They may be assaulting another inmate, using drugs, or trying to escape by removing bricks from the wall of one of the cells. You control the time, place, and duration of all conversations; don't allow yourself to be distracted from your duties. Although I am encouraging you to communicate with the inmates, I am strongly cautioning you to never lose sight of the fact that the inmates are not your friends. They are in jail for a reason—some for committing heinous and unthinkable crimes. Always remember that.

Don't Allow Your Personal Space to Be Invaded

When you are working and communicating with the inmates always be alert and do not allow them to invade your personal space. Don't let the inmates get too close to you. I would advise you not to let the inmates touch you either. Do not let an inmate put his hand on your shoulder while he is talking to you. That type of contact is improper and could be a prelude to an attack. Many officers have been injured by inmates that they allowed to get too close to them.

It is important for the inmates to maintain an appropriate distance and establish appropriate boundaries. In jail, it is common practice for officers to keep inmates at arm's length. That is the distance you would claim if you put your arm straight out in front of you and then turned around 360 degrees. You are not offending the inmates by doing this; they expect you to set boundaries. If an inmate gets too close to you, do not hesitate to tell him to step back.

Don't get into the habit of shaking hands with the inmates either. Some officers shake hands with inmates, but I have never felt comfortable doing it, so I would not advise anyone else to develop this habit. You don't have to shake an inmate's hand just because he extends his to you. Always make your personal safety your biggest priority and maintain the appropriate boundaries.

Never Discuss Your Private or Personal Life with Inmates

As I mentioned earlier the inmates are not your friends. Do not confide in the inmates and refrain from telling them personal information about yourself. Talking about your personal business is not part of the inmate-officer relationship. They can talk about their personal business with you, and in fact, that should be encouraged, but under no circumstances should you discuss your personal business with them.

Do not give inmates your personal information like your first name and do not tell them where you live because that information can be used against you. That is why officers should only refer to each other by their last names. I also advise officers to keep an unlisted telephone number. If an inmate knows your personal information *(i.e., your full name and where you live, telephone number, etc.)*, he may go to your home to seek revenge on you or your family if you have an altercation with him. Don't make it easy for them to locate you by giving them personal information. You can also have your identity stolen by giving your personal information to inmates. Inmates are not your friends.

Don't Tolerate Inappropriate Talk From Inmates

If an inmate talks to you in a disrespectful or sexually inappropriate manner do not tolerate it; notify your fellow officers and tell them word for word what the inmate said to you. Do not be ashamed. Your fellow officers will be supportive and assist you in dealing with those types of inmates. Do not be reluctant to write an inmate up by giving him an infraction if you deem it necessary. If you don't want to issue the inmate an infraction there are other ways to deal with disrespectful inmates that will be discussed later in the book. Either way, do not let an inmate get away with this type of abusive behavior.

Initially, inmates will test you. They want to see what you will and won't tolerate, so set the standard early. If you do not allow people to speak to you disrespectfully when you are outside the jail, do not let the inmates speak to you disrespectfully inside the jail.

One thing that you must always remember is that the inmates need you more than you need them. An inmate can't even get a roll of toilet paper without an officer's assistance. Use your leverage to maintain the level of respect that you require from the inmates. You have the upper hand, you have control, so when communicating with inmates, make sure they give you the proper respect.

KEY 2

BE FIRM, FAIR AND CONSISTENT

This will help to gain the respect of the inmates

To be a good and effective correction officer, you must gain the respect of the inmates. Once you gain the respect of the inmates you will find it easier to get the inmates to comply with your orders and instructions. In order to gain the respect of the inmates you must be firm, fair, and consistent.

Being Firm Means Standing Your Ground

There will be times when you will be at odds with an inmate or a group of inmates because you are enforcing the rules of the institution. You will feel pressured to abandon your position and go along with what the inmates want in order to avoid conflict. During these times remember, you are not trying to win a popularity contest. Your job is to enforce correction law and the rules that govern your institution. You must be firm—don't give in to the inmates in an attempt to win them over or to be popular. If the law and the rules are on your side, be resolute and maintain your position.

If the inmates feel that under pressure you will retreat from your position and give in to them, they will pressure you each and every time you make a decision until you give in. You will be an ineffective officer.

One officer can stand against an entire house of inmates if the officer is right and within the rules. The inmates will eventually realize that you cannot be moved from your position, and they will come around to your way of thinking. If you are enforcing the rules, you may not have the support of the majority of the inmates, but you will have the support of your fellow officers, captains, deputy wardens, and the warden, and they will come to your aid if you need assistance.

It is okay to listen to the inmates' concerns and, in some cases, even compromise with them when possible, but often you will have to draw the line in the sand and stand firm. If you can stand your ground in those types of situations, you will be on your way to gaining the respect of the inmates and your fellow officers.

Being Fair Means Don't Play Favorites

The rules should apply equally to every inmate regardless of race, education level, physical size, crime committed, sentence serving, etc.

You will often have inmates of different sizes, races, sexual orientations, or nationalities. You may even have inmates that speak a different language than your own. You may have the urge to favor the inmate or inmates with whom you have the most in common. Resist this urge. You cannot favor one inmate or group of inmates over the others. This will cause conflict among the inmates and cause the inmates that are not receiving special treatment to resent you. Be fair and treat the inmates equally. Treat them the way you would want to be treated if your situations were reversed.

For example, when you distribute personal care items like soap and toothpaste do so fairly. Be sure that all the inmates get an equal share. Don't give one group the supplies to distribute to the other inmates. Distribute the supplies yourself or closely supervise their distribution.

When you let an inmate or a group of inmates control the distribution of supplies or control the feeding unsupervised you create a two-tier system. You are sharing your power with that inmate or group, and that dilutes your power and authority.

Don't share your power with the inmates. Your power should remain consolidated with you—intact and undiluted. The inmates should know that you are the ultimate authority. You accomplish this by ensuring that each and every inmate is treated fairly. If you do these things, you will be on your way to gaining the trust and respect of the inmates.

Being Consistent Means Being Steady and Reliable

In a well-run jail there is an established daily routine. Services and programs happen on a schedule. However, a jail is only as good as its officers, so you, the officer, also must have a schedule and establish a routine. The inmates must become comfortable with the predictability of your routine. Although the time and frequency of your searches and security inspections should not be predictable, other aspects of your routine should be.

The inmates should be clear on what type of behavior you will and won't accept. Your demeanor should be consistent. Do not be moody or wishy-washy. When you take a position on an issue, your position should match your personality. That will make it easier to sustain your position over time.

For example, if you put a high value on cleanliness in your personal life, it will be easier for you to require that the inmates maintain a clean housing area. However, if you do not put a high value of cleanliness in your personal life, it will be difficult for you to require day in and day out that the inmates maintain a clean housing area.

Inmates will often test you to see if you are consistent. You will pass these tests by remaining consistent. Over time the inmates will become conditioned to accept your way of doing things.

When I was working on Riker's Island I didn't like to see the inmates sitting on the tables in the dayroom. The feedings were done in the dayrooms, and inmates would have to eat off these same tables. I felt it was very unsanitary for the inmates to sit on the tables.

When I first started working in the housing areas I would make the inmates get off the tables and tell them to sit in a chair instead. At first the inmates were very resistant to this and thought that I was just trying to boss them around. I explained to them that it was unsanitary to sit on tables that they later would have to eat off of.

Everyday when I came to work I would make them get

off the tables until they realized that I was serious and was not going to relent on this issue. After a while the inmates no longer sat on the tables and would go as far as to tell the new inmates that came to the housing area that they could not sit on the dayroom tables. I was able to be resolute in my position because I truly felt it was unsanitary to sit on the tables. I was consistent, and over time the inmates adapted to my way of doing things, which they eventually realized was in their best interest.

While I was assigned to one of the department's smaller commands I worked with an Officer Richards who weighed about 300 pounds. The housing area was small and held only about thirty inmates. He was almost always the biggest person in the housing area.

When all the inmates were smaller than him, which was most of the time, he ran the housing area with an iron fist. He enforced every rule. But when an inmate his size or bigger was admitted to his housing area, he would be lax about enforcing the rules and would let the bigger inmates get away with things that he never would let the smaller inmates get away with.

Officer Richards had developed a style of jailing that was based on intimidation of the smaller inmates. I would often talk to him about his style, telling him that he did not treat the inmates equally. If you want to enforce the rules to the letter then that's fine, but you can't stop enforcing them or get lax about enforcing them because someone in the housing area is your size or bigger. I often told him, "Stand for what you believe in, and if you feel that the rules should be strictly followed do not change your stance because of an inmate's size." I don't think I ever got through to him. All the big inmates thought Richards was cool while all the smaller inmates hated and despised him because they saw him as nothing more than a bully.

One day, the smaller inmates got together and planned to attack Richards. They persuaded one of the incorrigible inmates to attack Richards and promised him they all would jump in once he "set it off." The foolhardy inmate attacked Richards, but none of the other inmates helped him like they said they would. Richards beat the inmate to the ground and seriously injured him. The department determined that the force Richards used against the inmate was excessive and shortly after this incident Richards was transferred to a very large facility on Rikers Island.

In his new facility the housing areas were much larger and held many more inmates. His style of intimidating the smaller inmates did not go over well. He was jumped by the entire housing area several weeks after his transfer. He suffered many injuries, but more than his physical injuries, he suffered a blow to his self-esteem and confidence. His jailing style, which had worked for him in the smaller facility, had gotten him assaulted by his entire housing area at the larger facility. He became depressed and began using drugs. Six month after the incident he failed the department's drug test and was subsequently fired.

He was not firm, he was not fair, and he was not consistent. He locked himself into a style of jailing that was flawed, and his unwillingness to see the error of his ways led to his downfall. He never gained the respect of the inmates.

Key 3

How To Deal With Troublemakers

Approximately 10 percent of the inmates are truly troublemakers.

If you are new to corrections, you may think that all the inmates are troublemakers. That is not the case. From my experience I have found that only about 10 percent of the inmates are truly troublemakers. The other 90 percent just want to do their time without having too many problems with correction officers or other inmates.

So, if you have a housing area of sixty inmates, there will be approximately six inmates *(10 percent)* that are troublemakers. The other fifty-four inmates *(90 percent)* will not be a problem. For our purposes I will refer to these troublemakers as *Bad Onions.* I call them this because there are three layers of resentment that drive these inmates. Unfortunately, these Bad Onions usually have strong leadership qualities and can often influence some of the 90 percent to join them and cause problems, too.

In this chapter, we will discuss how to deal with these troublemakers and limit their influence on the other 90 percent. To do this we must first identify them and then understand why they are so resentful and at times hostile toward correction officers. First let me describe the Bad Onions so we can be clear on the type of inmate to which I am referring.

This is the inmate that is usually the most interested in what you are doing from the minute you enter the area. He will immediately make his presence known. He will want to make eye contact with you and give you dirty looks most of the time. If he's not sure about you he might put on a happy face and try to say something to you just to see how you react. He's trying to feel you out.

The other inmates will give you the once over and go back to their normal routine, but not this one. He watches you as you take your count and make your security inspections. You will often see him pointing you out to other inmates who are not concerned with you. He will begin to make you the focus of the other inmates.

This inmate will move more slowly than the others when you tell them to do something, or he just won't move at all. If you make a mistake, he will be the first one to point it out. He wants to show you what you are doing wrong and embarrass you in front of the other inmates. Even though you may try to avoid this inmate, you will realize early on that you and he are on a collision course.

If you are a female officer, this is the inmate that will call you the B word without reservation or hesitation. He is the one that will look you up and down in an attempt to make you feel like you don't belong here. If you are a male officer, he will position himself in your way or if he is smaller than you he may get another Bad Onion to assist him in his intimidation tactics. He really doesn't want to fight; he just wants to humiliate you and turn the other inmates against you. Whether you are male of female, he will find a way to disrespect you.

This inmate is clever. He will exploit any differences between you and your fellow officers. If you are new, he will appear to get along with the senior officers but not with you. If one officer is male and the other is female, he will listen to one but not the other. His goal is to divide the officers. He will take pleasure in any disagreement between the officers. And although he may act like he favors one officer over the other, he doesn't; he dislikes all officers equally.

When you first encounter this type of inmate you may ask yourself, "What did I do to him?" You didn't do anything to him. This is the way he is, so let's peel this onion and find out why, shall we?

The Three Layers of Resentment

The first layer of resentment stems from the fact that you are a man or woman with a future. You have a good job that pays a good salary. You are a peace officer with a shield and the legal right to carry a concealed firearm. These are things that this type of inmate will probably never have.

He thinks he knows how to do your job better than you do. In some areas his knowledge of the system may be greater than yours, but that's only because he has been in and out of jail most of his life. He is envious and resents the fact that you have authority over him and the other inmates, and wishes he had that authority. You represent what he may have been had he applied himself and taken a different path. Your presence is a constant reminder of his failure.

The second layer of resentment toward you is because you are a law enforcement officer. He feels the whole criminal justice system is corrupt and unfair and anyone who is a part of that system is also corrupt and unfair. He hates the fact that the criminal justice system has put him in jail and when he sees you in uniform you are the human manifestation of that system. He feels that he is the helpless victim of the system and as a result is unable to determine his own destiny.

The only way he can get any real satisfaction while in jail is by verbally and sometimes physically lashing out at the system, and in this case you represent the system. He is compelled to prove the system wrong therefore, he must prove you wrong. He feels the system is unfair so he must show everyone who will listen that you are unfair and what better place than in jail, where he has a captive audience.

In his mind, you represent the system, and he is the prosecutor, and the other inmates are the jury. Although he may be a drug dealer, murderer, or rapist, he feels that you are the enemy because you are depriving him of his ability to commit more crime and destruction. He doesn't see that it is his own behavior that has gotten him into this situation. He is projecting his frustration about himself and his situation on to you.

The third layer of the Bad Onion is the core. It is his resentment of authority that stems from childhood. These types of inmates usually had traumatic childhoods. Authority figures like parents or individuals in the foster care system abused them for most of their lives. Many have been the victims of physical, emotional, verbal, and even sexual abuse.

In addition, many of the men in jail have not had a father or a positive male role model in their lives during their formative years. A boy who grows up without a father or a positive male role model may develop resentment of authority at an early age. This is because the father represents authority in the mind of a male child. And if the boy doesn't know his father and never developed respect for his father or a male role model, he may have difficulty respecting any person in authority. The child may grow up to become an adult that rebels against any authority figure. This resentment is only compounded if the child's mother was abusive or neglectful.

In jail, you, as the correction officer, are the ultimate symbol of authority. Therefore, your presence alone is sufficient for these types of inmates to become hostile, uncooperative, and rebellious. These inmates have been betrayed, neglected, and abused by authority figures in the past and now, as adults, they want to hurt you before you hurt them.

So, How Do You Deal with These Types of Inmates?

In order to deal with these types of inmates and limit their influence on the other inmates, the officers assigned to an area must all work together. You must work as a team. You must communicate and make each other aware of the inmate or inmates that present a problem.

The most common way these Bad Onions successfully get away with disrespecting an officer and ultimately disrupting an area is by first dividing the officers. As stated earlier in this chapter, he does this by exploiting any differences between you and your fellow officers. He may appeal to one officer's ego and place him or her on a pedestal. Although he may pretend he favors one officer over the other, he doesn't. He dislikes all officers equally because you all represent the same thing—authority.

He must first divide the officers because he knows that he is going to need an officer's assistance at some point during the course of the day. He knows that he can't even get a roll of toilet paper or a tube of toothpaste without the help of an officer. Therefore, it is important for him to have at least one officer in the area that he can go to for assistance. You and your fellow officers cannot allow these divide-and-conquer techniques to be successful. If he is allowed to disrespect one officer and then go to another officer to get what he needs, there will be no reason for him to correct his disrespectful and disruptive behavior. This avenue of assistance must be cut off.

In order to resist being divided there must be communication and an understanding between the officers. It must be understood by every officer that if an inmate presents a problem for one officer, then he presents a problem for all the officers. There should be an agreement or pact between the officers to support one another.

The inmates should never see the officers arguing or loudly disagreeing with each other. If there are differences between the officers it should be discussed out of earshot of the inmates. The junior officers should defer to the senior officer when an agreement cannot be met.

When dealing with troublemakers or Bad Onions do not try to appease or pacify them in an effort to get them to behave. It doesn't help. It only makes their behavior worse.

Be sure to maintain your composure. Be professional and don't be argumentative. Do not let the inmate or inmates push your buttons and get you to overreact. Pick your battles, and do not get excited or upset over little inconsequential issues. Eventually, if the inmate continues on a disruptive path, he will commit a major violation and at that point you will have to confront him.

When you are having this confrontation with the inmate, all the officers should respond with a show of support, especially when that confrontation is with an inmate that has been identified as a troublemaker. The responding officers may not have to say anything; just being present and showing support often will help prevent the verbal confrontation from escalating into a physical altercation. It is also important for the senior officer to closely monitor these confrontations and/or verbal exchanges and intervene if necessary if the incident begins to escalate. The "A" officer should also be aware of what is going on and notify the captain if necessary. *(The "A" officer is the officer that controls who enters and exits the area. This officer also has access to the telephones and can contact the supervisor if needed.)*

The officers assigned to the area should handle these types of situations without the assistance of the captain whenever possible. If the captain responds to the area too often, an environment will be created where the inmates only behave when the captain is around. However, it is always a good idea to keep the captain informed when you are having problems so he is aware of what is going on. In the event that the confrontation escalates and the captain must be called to the area, he then would be fully informed concerning the problem to which he is responding.

When you have this inevitable confrontation with a Bad Onion, there is one more thing you must keep in mind—the Bad Onions are only about 10 percent of the inmate population. So, the battle for control does not revolve around winning over the 10 percent of troublemakers. The battle revolves around winning over the 90 percent that are not troublemakers. Some officers make the mistake of thinking that if they put the troublemakers in check, the rest of the inmates will fall in line. In theory this is correct, however, this course of action may have the opposite effect if executed improperly. If you are not careful, you may turn the remaining 90 percent against you.

The 90 percent know they have nothing to gain by having an ongoing conflict with an officer, especially their housing area officer. They know that when the officers are upset with the inmates, services slow to a crawl or are discontinued. But, this 90 percent will quickly side with the 10 percent if the officer is proven to be unfair or biased. If the officer doesn't handle the 10 percent correctly, the 90 percent will become frustrated with the officer's ineffectiveness, insensitivity, or lack of professionalism, and will turn on the officer and become allied with the 10 percent.

In a confrontation between you and the troublemaker, try not to get into a heated argument. But, if you find it necessary to argue, realize that what you say during this argument will either make or break you in the eyes of the other inmates.

Remember, you are the authority, and he and the other inmates know this. So, maintain your position and don't sink to the troublemaker's level. He may insult you and say things designed to provoke you to an all-out shouting match with him. When an officer falls for this and engages in this shouting match, he usually not only insults the troublemaker but the entire population of inmates, as well, by saying things like:

- *You're just an inmate.*
- *I'm going home in eight hours.*
- *You have to be here—I don't.*

When an officer allows the argument to sink to the level where he uses these or similar phrases, the officer has already lost the argument. As a result of making these types of statements the officer turns the 90 percent of inmates against him. Although, you are arguing with the troublemaker, you are telling the whole inmate population of that area how you feel about them.

Phrases like *You're just an inmate* cannot be directed to just one inmate because they all are inmates. You may be trying to put the troublemaker in his place, but what you have really done is confirm what the troublemaker is trying to convince the other inmates of. You have helped him prove that you don't care about any of them, and you feel that all inmates are less than human. You have also shown that you are unprofessional and do not deserve their respect and cooperation.

Phrases like *I'm going home in eight hours* or *You have to be here-I don't* have a similar effect. These are also phrases that cannot be directed toward one inmate. All the inmates are in the same predicament. They cannot go home, and they know that. Saying this during an argument is like rubbing salt in the wounds of every inmate in the area. It turns all the inmates against you, and that's what the troublemaker wants. You lose much of your respect by saying things like this, and the troublemaker grows in stature because he exposed you as an uncaring, insensitive officer. He becomes more powerful as you become less powerful.

The inmates that are watching wonder how you can deal with them fairly and according to their individual conduct if you already despise and dislike all inmates. You leave them little choice but to take the side of their fellow inmate whether he is right or wrong. Now it's inmate against officer, and you helped make that happen.

When you are confronting an inmate, keep your composure, remain professional, and try not to use profanity. When an officer uses profanity toward the inmates, he is also falling into the trap. He is giving up a degree of his moral authority. Now, he is stooping to the troublemaker's level. This is not the worst thing that the officer can do because inmates and officers often use profanity in jail. However, if the officer wants to take the moral high ground, he should refrain from using profanity.

If the troublemaker or any other inmate has violated a rule, keep the focus on that violation and tell him the consequences of violating the rule. If you keep your conversation focused on the individual inmate's behavior and not his status as an inmate you will get better results. You will also show the 90 percent who are onlookers that you are professional.

The 90 percent want the officers to win in these types of arguments because they don't want their services disrupted. They are rooting for you even though they can't admit it. They want the area to run smoothly, so don't ruin it for them and yourself by giving up your dignity, respect, and moral authority just to prove a point to a troublemaker. Your goal is to win over the 90 percent that are not troublemakers. The troublemakers will be forced to fall in line after you win over the 90 percent. Therefore, stand your ground, try not to argue, and remain professional.

Remember, jailing is not a one-on-one activity. It takes a team effort to maintain control of a jail. Communicate with your fellow officers and agree to support and protect one another. Don't be reluctant to reach out to your fellow officers for assistance or call your area supervisor if you deem it necessary.

You may encounter some supervisors that may attempt to discourage you from calling them when you have a problem with an inmate. Fortunately, these types of supervisors are few and far between. Most supervisors will welcome and encourage officers to call them if they need assistance. They understand that dealing with a problem at the early stages will prevent the problem from growing. They understand the value of officers and supervisors working as a team. A good supervisor, when called on, will assess the situation and take the appropriate action. He may reprimand or transfer the inmate or have you issue the inmate an infraction. Or he may counsel you on how to better deal with these types of inmates, but under no circumstances will a good supervisor belittle an officer for calling for assistance. So, if you feel you need assistance, then, by all means, call your area supervisor.

Another thing that officers do that erodes the respect inmates have for them and undermines their authority is giving inmates instructions or reprimanding them in a manner that embarrasses them. I have seen many officers develop a jailing style that includes yelling at inmates.

When you yell at an inmate you embarrass him in front of his peers. Even if you are right in giving instructions or a reprimand, the inmate will resent the way you singled him out and pointed out his mistakes to the others. The other inmates may sympathize with the inmate you are reprimanding and their respect for you will diminish. Refrain from yelling instructions across the room or reprimanding inmates so every other inmate can hear, whenever possible.

When I was assigned to the Queens Detention Complex, I worked in the Warden's Office. I discovered that wardens constantly received instructions from the chiefs and at times, reprimands as well. However, their instructions and reprimands were done in a professional manner. The chiefs took great care not to let the rest of the facility know that the warden was in error. The chiefs would never reprimand a warden in front of his command.

You wouldn't like it if the captain reprimanded you about your uniform in front of your peers at role call. You would prefer that he pulled you to the side before or after role call and spoke to you about it. It's more professional.

When you need to instruct or reprimand an inmate, walk up to him, and do it in a manner that will not be so noticeable to all the other inmates. You will get better results. If it is not an emergency and can be done at another time, when the other inmates are not around, wait for that time to tell the inmate of his mistake.

A good time to talk to an inmate about his behavior is when he asks you for something. For example, if an inmate asks you if he can go to the commissary, that is a good time to speak to him about his behavior. You can answer by saying, "Yeah, you can go to the commissary and by the way, I saw you throw those papers on the floor earlier. So, clean those up, and then I will call the commissary for you." He will be more receptive to your instructions and will appreciate that you didn't yell at him in front of everyone. This is a good and effective way to correct unwanted inmate behavior.

I often would have conditions attached to honoring inmates' requests. For example, if I noticed earlier in the tour that an inmate had been too loud and boisterous during breakfast, I would remind him of his unacceptable behavior when he asked me for something. I would tell him that I would honor his request but during lunch, he would have to tone it down.

This way you are not just reprimanding the inmate, you're helping him with something and in return you are asking him to help you by controlling his behavior. If you do this during the course of your day, you will have a positive influence on the 90 percent that you are trying to win over. You also will be creating a better living environment for the inmates and a better working environment for yourself and your fellow officers.

If you conduct yourself in a professional manner, help the 90 percent with their daily needs, and set a standard of acceptable conduct with those that ask you for assistance, the troublemakers will be powerless against you. The other inmates will not listen to their complaints about you because you are helping to improve their jail experience. The troublemakers will be exposed for trying to add more stress to an already stressful situation.

Now, you have won, and the troublemakers have lost. You have solidified your position of authority and gained the respect of the 90 percent. Now the troublemakers are isolated and separated from the rest. Now, the troublemakers will become more compliant and less problematic.

KEY 4

LEARN HOW TO SAY "NO"

Don't let inmates intimidate you into allowing them to do things that they are not suppose to do.

When you are working in a jail, you may have to supervise dozens of inmates, each with his own set of problems. When you first become a correction officer, inmates will ask you for permission to do things that they know are against the rules. This is called the "feeling-out process." The inmates want to test you to see what you will and won't allow them to do. This also happens to experienced officers when they work with a new set of inmates.

Most of the inmates already know the rules because many of them have been coming to jail since they were nineteen years old, and before that, many of them were in juvenile facilities. So, they know how the system works. They also know that some officers will look the other way and allow them to do things that are not permitted because they don't know the rules, are intimidated and afraid to stand up to the inmates, or just too lazy and uncaring to enforce the rules. They want to know what type of officer you are. Will you tell them no when you are suppose to or will you tell them yes and look the other way?

Don't let the inmates intimidate you into allowing them to do things that they are not suppose to do. You are a correction officer, and your job is the care, custody, and control of the inmates. What we are discussing here is the control aspect of the job. If you can't tell the inmates no when they want to break the rules, then you are not controlling the inmates. The inmates are controlling you. If you are not willing to control the inmates, then you are not fulfilling your duty as a correction officer.

You will have to tell the inmates no at some point, and they will get upset with you about it. That is all part of the job. You can't make everyone happy all the time. But that's okay. Inmates can be upset with you and respect you at the same time. However, you cannot allow them to walk all over you and expect them to respect you.

During the feeling-out process let the inmates know that you are going to be the type of officer that is going to enforce the rules. Let them know that you intend to exercise control over them—not as a bully or a tyrant but as a professional correction officer. The law gives you that authority, but it is up to you to use it and assert it when necessary. Maintain that standard throughout your career, and you will earn the respect and compliance of the inmates.

Stroking

One other practice that deserves mentioning when talking about control is stroking. Stroking is when an officer prom ises an inmate or a group of inmates something but has no real intention of doing what was promised, or when an officer leads an inmate to believe something that is entirely untrue. This falls in the category of control because it is a technique used by the officers to control the inmates. However, I discourage any officer from using this practice.

An officer should be of good moral character. An officer should be honest, reliable, and trustworthy no matter what type of inmates he is assigned to work with. Just because inmates use lies and deception to get what they want is not justification for officers to apply similar practices. As an officer, when you give your word, be true to your word. Don't use lies and deception as a tool to control inmate behavior. This is not a good practice and can cause unexpected problems.

The following is an *example* of an officer who strokes an inmate to punish him for being disrespectful.

On Friday, when Officer Brown told inmate James Taylor to go into his cell for the three o'clock count, Taylor replied, "F#*k you, Brown. I'm not going in my cell. GO TO HELL!" Taylor eventually went into his cell, but Officer Brown decided that he would get back at Taylor later for being disrespectful.

So the next day, which was Saturday, inmate Taylor was expecting his wife and children to visit him. So, he got up early, showered, shaved, and put on his best clothes and sat in the dayroom waiting to be called to the visit area. Two hours went by, and he began to wonder whether his wife and children had made it to the jail. So, he said to Officer Brown, "Officer Brown, can you call the visit house for me and see if my wife and kids are here yet?"

"Yeah, sure I'll call," Officer Brown replied. However, Officer Brown was still holding a grudge from the day before. He remembered that Taylor told him "F#*k you, Brown, I'm not going in my cell. GO TO HELL!" He couldn't get those words out of his head, and now it was Brown's chance to get even.

Officer Brown let Taylor see him get on the phone and make what appeared to be a call to the visit area. But in reality Brown was calling his friend in the housing area across the hall. Then after this fictitious telephone conversation, he told Taylor that his wife and kids were not in the visit area yet.

A half hour later, Taylor's wife and kids were in the visit area. However, when the visit area called for Taylor, Officer Brown answered the phone and told the visit area that Taylor was not in the housing area. He said Taylor had gone to the clinic. When the visit area called back thirty minutes later, Brown told them that Taylor had gone to commissary. When they called back again twenty minutes later, he told them that Taylor had gone to the yard. All the while Taylor was sitting in the dayroom waiting to be called. Taylor's wife and kids just sat and waited until they got tired of waiting and eventually left.

This is generally how a classic stroke job works. An officer tells an inmate he is going to do something for him but has no real intention of doing it. In this case, Officer Brown led Taylor to believe that he was calling the visit area when he wasn't.

Some may see what Officer Brown did to Taylor as a harmless prank or feel that Taylor deserved this treatment. However, I disagree. Yes, Taylor was disrespectful to Officer Brown the day before, but Brown did not have to stoop to his level. When he was asked by Taylor to call the visit area, Officer Brown should have just said NO! And if Taylor wanted to know the reason why, Officer Brown should have told Taylor he was not calling because he disrespected him the day before.

Of course initially Taylor is going to get upset, but now he knows the truth. This is a better response because it will cause Taylor to reflect on his previous behavior and may cause him to change his ways in the future. This way Brown takes the moral high ground and doesn't become mired in lies and deceptions. He maintains his respectability, which will aid him when dealing with Taylor and other inmates in the future.

When officers make stroking a part of their jailing style, it undermines their efforts to gain the inmates' trust and respect. It also heightens the level of distrust and resentment inmates harbor toward officers in general. Over time, stroking can create a dangerous work environment for all officers. Let me give you an example of what I mean.

Let's go back to inmate Taylor. He never received his visit. At 6:00 P.M. he called his wife at home. He thought that maybe something happened to her and their three children on the way to visit him. He found out that she got all three kids up at 7:00 A.M., dressed them in their Sunday best and spent two hours on a bus to Rikers Island. Then when they arrived, they waited on line for another hour to register. After being searched, she and the kids sat at a visit table for nearly an hour waiting for him to come down to the visit area.

Taylor told her that he had been sitting in the dayroom waiting for the visit area to call for him since 8:00 A.M. and that Officer Brown called the visit area and was told that no one had arrived. She told Taylor that the visit officer called his housing area, but the housing area officer said he was out to the clinic, then the commissary, and then the yard. She told Taylor that after waiting for nearly an hour, the kids were all hungry and irritable so they left and went back home.

As Taylor heard this story from his wife, he realized exactly what happened. Officer Brown lied about calling the visit area. Then he told the visit officer that he was out. Taylor got angry about what Officer Brown had done to him and his family. Even though Taylor recalled that he did in fact disrespect Officer Brown the day before, he felt that he should not have taken it out on his wife and innocent children. Taylor is now very angry!

Officer Brown, who did the stroke job on Taylor, is long gone; you relieved him at 3:30 P.M. Now you are the officer in the housing area. Taylor was so angry that after he finished talking to his wife, he slammed the telephone down and broke the receiver.

Immediately, all the other inmates jumped up because they realized their telephone, their only link to the outside world, had been broken. Now, none of them can make phone calls for the rest of the evening, and the phone may not be fixed until Monday. The other inmates began arguing with Taylor, and were about to jump him and beat the hell out of him for breaking the phone. Before they did, he apologized and told them what Officer Brown did to him and his wife and kids.

Now, here you come, the innocent officer who didn't have anything to do with what happened that morning. You weren't even in the building that morning. You hear the commotion and go over to investigate. You get to the crowd of inmates that are arguing near the phone and raise your voice to say, "Hey, what's going on?" That's all it takes for the wrath of the inmates to be directed toward you. And you don't even have a clue of what's happening.

In the introduction to this book I told you that, "Once you put on that uniform and step into that jail you are a correction officer, 100 percent." What one officer does may cause problems for you. So, take an interest in what your fellow officers are doing and how they conduct themselves. You are all connected, you are a unit. The inmates usually will not take the time to distinguish between the officers when they set it off [a riot]. They see you in that uniform and at that moment, you are the enemy. If officers in your jail are constantly stroking inmates and have a problem with being honest and saying no, then your jail is a pressure cooker, a time bomb ready to explode.

Conduct yourself as a professional, stand for what's right, and be honest with the inmates. Require that your fellow officers do the same. If you develop a jailing style that has truth and honesty at its core, the inmates and your fellow officers will know you are real and will respect you. The officers won't conduct themselves in an unprofessional manner when they know you will be involved. It will be easier for the inmates to make the distinction between you and the officers that are stroking them and maybe they will have enough respect for you not to harm you if they decide to set it off.

If you promise the inmates something, make sure you fulfill your promise. Don't forget because the inmates will remember. You have a memo book to help you remember, so write things down so you don't forget. This is a good way to establish good rapport with the inmates. The inmates will respect you if you are true to your word. Your housing area may have seventy, eighty, or more inmates. Most of them will ask you for something or will ask you to do something for them. If you're going to do it, then remember it and get it done. If you know you won't or can't do it, then tell them NO!

Breaking the Rules

Inmates will often ask you to bend or even break the rules. Just tell them NO. If they don't know what they are asking is against the rules explain that to them. If after that, an inmate tells you, "Well, Officer Jones lets us do it," then tell him to wait until he sees Officer Jones and get him to do it.

Inmates will often tell you that another officer has bent this rule or broken that rule when they are trying to get you to break the rules. And you know what? There are times when they are telling the truth. I have seen some officers bend the rules or break the rules, sometimes out of ignorance and sometimes because it is more convenient to do so.

An example of bending or breaking the rules may be something simple like letting the inmates run the telephones unsupervised, letting them handle cleaning supplies unsupervised, or letting them have unfettered access to the supply closet. It may be convenient for you to allow inmates to do these things but, it can prove to be problematic. If a fight breaks out over the telephone or someone gets assaulted with ammonia, a mop ringer, or a scrub brush from the supply closet, you may find yourself in big trouble for bending the rules.

So, if you're being asked to bend or break a rule, just say no. You have enough to worry about without having to stick your neck out for the inmates. There's a saying in jail that goes *It's all good, until it's not.* Which means that everything is fine until something goes wrong. And in a jail things can go wrong.

In addition, just like that inmate told you that *"Officer Jones lets us do it,"* when things go wrong, that inmate is going to tell everyone who will listen that *"Officer Jones lets us do it."* If you don't want to be that Officer Jones, then learn how to say NO!

If an inmate asks you to let him do something, and you don't know whether it is permissible or not, ask another officer. And if you realize that the officer you are asking doesn't know either, call the supervisor. Never take the inmate's word in questionable situations, always verify.

KEY 5

DON'T HOLD GRUDGES

Holding grudges against inmates is like carrying around a bag of bricks. Learn to let it go.

Every now and then you will encounter an inmate or a group of inmates that are very irritating and just gets on your nerves. They seem to be ungrateful and do things that don't make sense. The following is an example of a series of events that may lead to an officer holding a grudge against a group of inmates like these.

On this day everything seemed to be going quite well until the end of the tour. It was lock-in time, and the inmates refused to lock in, which caused the institutional count to be delayed. As a result, Officer Allen got out of work late, which caused her to miss her dental appointment. So she vowed that the next time she had that housing area she was going to get those inmates back.

She replayed her entire tour of duty over in her mind and recalled all the things she had done for those inmates. She pulled a few strings and called in a couple of favors from her friends that worked in the commissary to have her housing area called to the commissary first, to make sure all the good snacks would not be sold out when they got there. She took part of her lunch break to go down to the jail storehouse to get soap and toothpaste for the inmates because there was none left in the housing area, and the storehouse officers were too busy to deliver the items. She even was able to call around and get them a working fan to replace the broken one in the back of the housing area. Then when it was time for Officer Allen to go home, the inmates acted up and refused to lock in, which caused her to get out of work late and miss her dental appointment, which she had been waiting three weeks for.

On her way home all she could think of was ways to get those inmates back. Instead of relaxing when she got home, she plotted what she was going to do to those inmates when she got back to work tomorrow. Maybe she would return the fan or just maybe she would turn the television's circuit breaker off right in the middle of their favorite show just to get them back and show them who was boss. Nighttime came and instead of sleeping, she was still plotting and planning how she would teach those inmates a lesson that they would never forget. She even came up with special things to do to the ringleaders. She remembered that some of the inmates would be out to court when she got there tomorrow and determined that she would get them back the day after tomorrow. This line of thinking escalated and as she grew increasingly angry, she became more determined than ever to get the inmates back and show them who was running things.

I'm here to tell you to let it go. Do not hold grudges and don't waste your time plotting how to get back at inmates that you feel disrespected you. Don't take your job home with you and don't lose any sleep over what inmates do. I know it is not easy, but for your own good, it is better not to hold grudges. Holding grudges against inmates is like carrying around a bag of bricks. Your job is stressful enough without carrying around old grudges. In addition, don't go overboard when you put inmates on the burn.

On the Burn

On the burn is a term used in jail that means denying the inmates something that they have become accustomed to. For example: an officer may put inmates on the burn by not allowing them to make extra phone calls or restricting phone calls to the legal minimum of six minutes. There are many things officers can do to burn inmates and make their stay in jail a living hell. I won't list them because inmates may get copies of this book. Furthermore, these techniques, although necessary to maintain control, can be extremely harmful to the safety of the institution if they are not practiced correctly. It would be irresponsible for me to publish these techniques. Officers should learn how and when to put the inmates on the burn from senior officers and personal experience.

If you must burn an inmate or inmates, contain the burn to your tour. Once you get relieved don't pressure your relief officer to continue burning the inmates. Just tell your relief officer what occurred during your tour and let him determine if he wants to pick up from where you left off.

It should be the relieving officer's decision. If you want to burn the inmates the next day when you return to work, that's your choice.

I am appealing to the officer that is being relieved because most officers are loyal to their fellow officers and would continue to burn the inmates if asked to. I think loyalty is extremely important, so I'm asking the officer being relieved not to burden the next officer. Let him run his tour the way he sees fit.

I never liked to burn inmates on my tour for what they did on the previous tour unless they did something really foul like assault an officer. I always wanted to treat the inmates according to the way they behaved on my tour. Then if they misbehaved, I would deal with them in my own way during my tour. I wouldn't tell my relief officer to continue burning the inmates on his tour.

I've seen times when episodes of burning inmates have gone on for days and weeks with one officer passing it on to the next. This continuous burn is not good for the officers or the safety of the institution. It keeps the inmates in a constant state of unrest. It also puts more stress on the officers and may cause a disturbance or riot.

I know there are exceptions to every rule. Occasionally you will find some housing areas that are filled with problematic inmates that deserved to be burned all day, everyday. In extreme cases like those, I suggest that the housing area officers work with the area captains and assistant deputy warden (ADW) to come up with a better way of dealing with problematic inmates. Separating those inmates by transferring some of them to other housing areas or different jails may be a solution.

The whole idea behind burning the inmates is to compel them to comply with your instructions. However, if you burn them too often, it loses its effectiveness. It will make your job more stressful, which is the opposite of its intended purpose.

You don't have to burn the inmates for every little thing they do wrong. Learn how to forgive, and look at each day as a new day, not a continuation of yesterday. Give the inmates a new opportunity to do better tomorrow.

For those of you who believe in God or another higher power, think about it this way. God wakes you up every day even if you did something wrong the day before. He gives you another twenty-four hours to do better. If you don't do better the next day, he wakes you up again and gives you yet another twenty-four hours to get it right. Now, if God were the type to hold grudges, none of us would live to see tomorrow.

Give the inmates another chance to do better. They make mistakes just like you do. Inmates and officers alike sometimes say and do things that they later regret. Don't go overboard when you have the upper hand. Treat the inmates the way you would want to be treated if your situations were reversed.

If you intend to have a long career in corrections, realize that you will be seeing many of the same inmates throughout your career. Unfortunately, many inmates are recidivist, and will be in and out of jail throughout their entire lives. Many of the inmates that I encountered in 1987, when I started in corrections were still getting arrested and coming back to jail when I left corrections in 2005. I have worked with many of the same inmates throughout my career. I have seen inmates grow up and get older in the system, and they have seen me do the same.

Ten or fifteen years from now you will be reminiscing with these same inmates that you are having problems with today. You will look back at these times as "the good ole days," and you will have a good laugh. So, don't hold grudges. Learn to forgive, turn the page and move on to the next adventure.

When you get relieved, go home, and leave all the problems of the jail at the jail. Don't lose any sleep over it. Don't remain in that stressful state because the stress that you won't let go of will cause you to be irritable and short tempered with your family and friends. It will eventually cause you medical problems and might kill you. So, don't hold grudges—let it go.

One of the things that I found to be helpful was not to wear my uniform home when I had a stressful day at work. I would leave the uniform in my locker and symbolically leave all the stress of the day in the uniform. If I was taking the uniform home to be cleaned, I would put it in a bag and take it home. I wouldn't wear it home.

Note concerning uniforms: *You should not wear your uniform home after working in the jail primarily for hygienic reasons. When you wear your uniform home from work, you are transferring the germs that are on that uniform to your car and to your home. You don't want to take the germs* *from work home with you. That is one of the major reasons uniforms and lockers were invented.*

Sometimes when we are in a hurry to go home, we throw our coats on over our uniforms and leave the jail. Everyone does this sometimes, but you shouldn't make it a habit. Don't take the germs that are in the jail home to your family.

I think this problem doesn't only relate to corrections but to many professions that are required to wear uniforms. Doctors, nurses, nurses' aides, and other health care workers wear their uniforms on the trains and buses to and from work. This is not healthy for the patients.

Many of the things I am telling you not to do in these chapters I have done myself and have learned that they don't work. I'm trying to help you save time by learning from my mistakes. Every officer wants to reach the point in his career where he is at peace with himself. The point where there is a balance of mind, body, and spirit, and a balance between you the officer and you the person. Some officers take many years to achieve this balance. Some officers never achieve it. The ones that never achieve a balance are the ones that are always getting into fights and arguments with the inmates and other officers. They are the ones that are always being written up by their supervisors. These are the ones that have strife and turmoil in their personal lives and will be prone to getting arrested outside the job. They are the ones that won't make it to retirement. You have the power to determine the tenor of your career and of your life.

KEY 6

CONTROL YOUR TEMPER

Before you can control others, you must first be in control of yourself.

An officer named Harrison once gave me some very good advice. She told me the following: "Don't come to work angry or stressed out. Let the inmates build your temper." These words of wisdom stuck with me my entire career. Now, I want to pass them on to you.

Let the Inmates Build Your Temper

Think of your temper as a scale from one to ten, with one being no temper and ten being red hot with anger. If you come to work with a temper level of five or six, you don't have very far to go before you're at ten. Any little thing an inmate does is going to set you off, and you're going to be arguing or fighting. We don't want that. If you come to work with your temper at one or two, you won't be so angry when things go wrong. And if, during the course of your day, your temper does get up to ten, well, you know that the inmates took you there. Your anger is warranted because you didn't come to work like that. And you know what? Usually, during your tour you won't get to ten. By the time you get to seven or eight, your tour will be over, and it will be time to go home.

KEY 7

TRY NOT TO ARGUE

Inmates who are stressed out and miserable want to see you miserable too. You have the power to determine whether to engage in an arguments.

Jail is full of stressed out, angry, and argumentative inmates. One inmate may be angry because he thought he was going to be found innocent and be released from jail but instead was found guilty and was sentenced to ten years behind bars. Another may be angry because her boyfriend let her drive his car to the store but didn't tell her that there were drugs in the trunk. After the police pulled her over and arrested her for drug trafficking, she called her boyfriend who told her that he would bail her out and tell the police that the drugs were his. That was three weeks ago, and everyone she calls tells her that her boyfriend has left town. Another inmate may be frustrated and angry because his wife, who vowed she would stick by him while he is in jail, didn't visit him this week and when he called the house another man answered the phone and told him not to call there anymore.

Many inmates have stories like these. These inmates are stressed out and miserable and would like to see you miserable, too, because misery loves company. No one becomes a correction officer with the goal of becoming like the inmates he supervises, but it happens. It's not a deliberate process. It is a gradual process. That's what you have to guard against.

When I first became a correction officer I got into arguments with inmates nearly every day. I had three fights in the first two months. I was becoming stressed out. I was losing sleep and becoming very argumentative at work and in my personal life. I began to become disillusioned with the idea of being a correction officer.

Then as the weeks went on I began to notice that there were some very good and effective officers that hardly ever argued or fought with the inmates. I saw that these officers didn't appear to be stressed out. I began to observe these officers closely and realized that these officers were problem solvers, and they were proactive not reactive. They knew how to recognize and defuse problems before they got to the boiling point. These officers didn't dread coming to work; they looked at their jobs as a daily challenge. I realized I could choose to be like those officers. So, I began to model my jailing style after those types of officers.

I became aware that I was in control of how my day was going to go, not the inmates. Thereafter, before I would leave my house to go to work I would say to myself, *"I am going to have a good day today, and I am not going to argue with anyone."* As I rode the bus across the Rikers Island bridge, I would repeat those words to myself. Almost instantly the amount of arguments I had during the course of my day went down.

Each week thereafter I had fewer and fewer arguments and not one fight because most fights began with an argument. During that time in my career I began to realize that I had the power to determine what type of experience I was going to have. I took the power away from the inmates.

I began using my communication skills to get compliance from the inmates. I learned how to listen and how to recognize a problem before it got to the boiling point. I became proactive instead of reactive. I began using my authority not to demand that inmates do things my way but to guide the inmates in the direction I wanted them to go—a direction that was also in their best interest. I began to lead by example.

I became a problem solver. I learned what the inmates' problems were and when possible, I helped them solve them. I began to learn the different areas of the jail so I could be a more knowledgeable officer. I would volunteer to work in the receiving room, movement control, visits, the storehouse, and other important areas in an effort to increase my knowledge of the jail. This made me a better officer in the eyes of the inmates and my fellow officers because I understood how the areas of the jail were interrelated.

During your career, you will see many different types of officers; some will be more skilled and effective than others. Don't hesitate to adopt some of the ways and techniques of the skillful officers. However, what works for one officer may not necessarily work for you. So, don't get discouraged; it takes time to develop a jailing style that works for you. Be observant and ask questions, and before you know it you will know how to deal with each and every situation you may encounter in jail.

Key 8

Use Your Instincts

Think of your instincts as an early warning system.

We live in the most technologically advanced time in human history. Everyday there's some new technological breakthrough. Our cities are getting bigger. We have gotten so far away from nature that many of us have forgotten how to survive without our technology. I'm not saying that technology is a bad thing—hell, I'm typing this book on a laptop computer. The point I'm trying to make is that we are human beings, and human beings are part of the animal kingdom. We are mammals just like your cat or dog, just like a lion or tiger. All animals have instincts, including human beings. Think of your instincts as an early warning system.

If you are afraid of a dog, the dog knows it instinctively. If your intentions are to harm him, he knows that too, even before you raise your hand to strike. Animals can sense fear and danger, and in the wild they use those instincts to survive. You, believe it or not, have these same instincts. However, because we are very rarely if ever put in a situation where we must use them to survive, they lay dormant. They get weak, but they never entirely leave us.

You may be walking alone at night and sense danger, but you don't see anyone nearby. So, you rationalize that your fear is not real and that the danger doesn't exist, and you continue on your path. Sometimes you may cross the street or take a different route to your destination. These are your instincts alerting you, warning you of potential danger. We have conditioned ourselves to ignore these urges.

If you aspire to be a good correction officer you must learn to reconnect with your instincts. You must heighten your sensitivity to them and trust them. If you sense danger don't rationalize it away. The danger may be real. Trust how you feel, and if you sense danger, stay alert and vigilant, and watch your back until the feeling subsides. Your instincts are there to help you survive. They are your early warning system.

An experienced correction officer can walk into a room full of inmates and sense the mood of that room. If there is tension, he can feel it. Often, in jail everything will appear normal before violence breaks out. Visually, there may not be any signs to alert you that something is wrong, but a good correction officer will sense that something is amiss. This is because he is in tune with his inner self. He has a heightened sense of awareness that will alert him to danger.

You must learn how to use your instincts; your life may depend on it. Humans have survived and prospered on earth for thousands of years not because of technology but because of our survival instincts. Reconnect with yours, and they will keep you safe.

KEY 9

VIOLENCE

Self-preservation is the first law of nature.
Always defend yourself.

I was twenty-two years old when I became a correction officer, and like most twenty-two-year-olds, I thought I was invincible. I had a gung-ho attitude and often threw caution to the wind when confronting inmates. Sometimes you find yourself in situations where you must take action, and where you must use force to defend yourself or someone else. But at times I wonder if some of those instances in which I was involved when force was used could have been avoided if I had known then what I know now.

It took most of my career to develop my rationale concerning using force. Although I have no permanent injuries related to my service, I have had my share of battle scars. I have spent time in hospital emergency rooms with injuries and have visited many of my fellow officers who were also injured in the line of duty.

When you're in that emergency room after a use-of-force incident, you go over in your mind the series of events that got you or your fellow officers injured. Most of the time you conclude that there was nothing you or anyone else could have done to prevent what happened, but on rare occasions you can see exactly what went wrong and who among you overreacted or antagonized the inmate(s) a little too much. What I'm trying to say to you officers and prison guards is simple: use your head, not your brawn to solve problems whenever you can. Using physical force to compel inmates to comply with the rules should not be your first option.

Using physical force as the first option is not sustainable over time. It may work when you're twenty-two years old, but will it work when you're thirty-two or forty-two years old and the inmates you are dealing with are nineteen or twenty years old? How long can you continue to engage in physical altercations and come out unscathed? It stands to reason that the more use-of-force incidents you are involved in, the more you expose yourself to the possibility of being injured. So, your goal should be to keep all use-of-force incidents to a minimum.

Now, by no means am I implying that you refrain from defending yourself. Always defend yourself. It's better to be judged by twelve than carried by six.* But be wise about when and how you use force.

Another factor that you must keep in mind when using force is your potential exposure to infectious diseases. The potential exposure to viruses like HIV or hepatitis increase when you come in contact with blood. Many inmates are infected with these viruses and may not even know it.

**It's better to be judged by twelve, than carried by six. This saying means: It's better to go to court and be judged by a jury of twelve and have the opportunity to explain your actions than to be killed and carried in a coffin by six pallbearers.*

For example: If you get into a physical altercation with an inmate who has the HIV virus, and if you punch him in the mouth and he starts bleeding, you run the risk of contracting HIV. It is not uncommon to receive a cut or laceration on your fist by punching someone in the mouth. Your fist can easily be cut on the other person's tooth. Now, you have an open wound through which the inmate's blood can penetrate your body.

Don't risk your health and well-being if it is not absolutely necessary. Violence is like a wild fire: it spreads fast, and it's hard to put out. I've witnessed many use-of-force incidents, as well as inmate fights that start with a few cross words and end in a bloody mess. Think before you leap and allow cooler heads to prevail.

When I worked on Riker's Island in A.M.K.C. (C-95) there was a period that almost everyday we had a problem with one of the inmate housing areas. The inmates would barricade themselves in their housing area by piling chairs and tables against the gates to protest some perceived mistreatment and dare us officers to come in and do battle with them. And each time we would march down to the housing area where the disturbance was taking place. We would respond in waves of twenty or more all suited up with riot vests, helmets, and batons led by a deputy warden.

We'd stand at the door of the housing area in full view of the protesting inmates in formation twenty and sometimes forty officers deep, all champing at the bit and itching to rush in to do battle with them. Then the deputy warden would go into the housing area and negotiate with the leaders of the protest while we stood in the corridor.

We would stand there waiting for the signal to attack. After about fifteen or twenty minutes the deputy warden would emerge from his conference with the inmate leaders and tell us that everything was settled, and the inmates would take down the barricades. While we stood in the corridor the deputy warden always gave us a speech about why he negotiated with the inmates. He said, "It was better for me to negotiate with the inmates than to have to explain to one of your families that you got seriously injured or killed taking back control of a housing area from the inmates."

Most of us that were suited up in riot gear felt that what the deputy warden was saying was a copout and maybe he was scared of going to battle with the inmates, but we weren't. We wanted to break through those barricades and teach those inmates a lesson.

As I got older and wiser I realized that the deputy warden was absolutely right. My fellow officers and I, who wanted to go to battle, were wrong. The deputy warden wasn't coping out; he was acting responsibly. He knew that it was better to use whatever legal and ethical tools at his disposal to get the outcome that he wanted without using force. When you use force you risk getting people on both sides hurt.

I've been on riot squads that were allowed to take back housing areas by force and almost every time officers and inmates were injured. I have concluded that it is always better if cooler heads prevail. Take a long-term view of your career in corrections; if you expect to have a long career and make it to retirement, you have to be smart. Don't use force if you can find another way to get the desired results.

Most inmates are not troublemakers and want to comply with the rules, but they also want to be respected. They don't want to lose face or be punked in front of the other inmates. If you give them a way out of a sticky situation that doesn't include violence, they will usually take it. However, if you back them into a corner with no other options, they will fight no matter what the odds are. The smallest mouse, if backed into a corner with all avenues of escape cut off, will fight you to the death. However, if you leave him an avenue of escape no matter how small the avenue, he will chose to escape rather than fight. You don't have to always go to blows with the inmates to get them to do what you want.

Whenever I talk with officers about showing restraint I'm always concerned that I will be misinterpreted, so let me take this opportunity to make myself perfectly clear. Always defend yourself; self-preservation is the first law of nature. Never, ever let an inmate assault you. If you feel that you are in imminent danger of being attacked do not wait to be struck before you take action. I don't care what directive your department gives you. Don't ever let a rule, regulation, or directive prevent you from defending yourself if you feel that your life is in danger.

Often law enforcement departments issue guidelines that are ambiguous and confusing about when to and when not to use force. I think they do this for two reasons: the first reason is that many of the policies are written primarily by lawyers that have no idea of what really goes on in a jail. The second reason is the department wants to keep the number of use-of-force incidents to a minimum in order to decrease the legal liability the department will face. If the rank and file officer is confused about when to and when not to use force, the officers will be reluctant to use force and the net result will be less use-of-force incidents.

Don't let their lack of knowledge of the way things are in jail or their desire to absolve the department of all liability cause you to be injured or killed. If you fear for your life strike first, strike hard, and strike fast. If you were walking down the street and someone got in your face, and you feared for your life, you wouldn't wait for the person to strike you before you decided to defend yourself. So, don't come to jail and let an inmate strike you.

Use whatever force is necessary to protect and defend yourself, and continue to use the appropriate force to terminate the incident. This means that when the inmate stops fighting back, you stop fighting also. If the inmate stops fighting, and you continue striking him, then you become the attacker. At that point you are no longer defending yourself, you have become the aggressor. Do not cross that line.

Why We Use Force

For a correction officer, violence is an occupational hazard. Sometimes in order to control inmates, correction officers must use violence. We refer to violence that we are in control of as force. Force is one of the tools that we have at our disposal to compel inmates to comply with our orders. For example, we can use force to defend ourselves or others. If an inmate is suppose to go to court today but refuses to go, we may use force to make that inmate go to court. If it's lock-in time, and the inmates refuse to go into their cells, we can use force to make them go into their cells. And if the court orders an inmate to submit to a DNA test, and he refuses, we can use force to assist the medical examiner in getting a blood sample.

This is a form of violence, but we try to limit and control it. We realize that violence or the use of force is a part of our job. We understand that sometimes you must use violence to combat violence in the same way firefighters sometimes must use fire to fight fire.

We'd rather not use force to get compliance, but when you are dealing with the segment of the population that society says must be locked behind metal gates and electrified fences, you expect that you will have to use force from time to time.

Everyday, when you watch the news, I'm sure you see people being arrested for perpetrating horrendous acts of violence. Just yesterday I saw on the news a man who was taken into custody for killing and decapitating a twenty-four-year-old female hiker in Georgia. He confessed to the murder and took police to the woman's body in return for the district attorney (DA) not seeking the death penalty. This monster will be in jail for the rest of his life.

In a week or two, he will no longer be on television and most people will forget about him and move on with their lives, and the police that caught him will move on to another case. But, in Georgia there is a group of correction officers that will have to deal with this monster every day and night for the rest of his life.

Just because he was caught and put in jail doesn't mean that he is no longer dangerous. He doesn't become a model citizen just because he was caught. If he has been killing people and stashing their bodies in the woods for the last fifteen or twenty years, he doesn't miraculously lose the urge to kill. The only thing standing in his way is that group of correction officers in Georgia. If allowed to, he will escape. Or he will injure or kill his fellow inmates or a correction officer if the opportunity presents itself.

We correction officers are law-abiding citizens with families. We have children that depend on us to provide for them. We can't afford to lose control of our inmates. We can't give them the opportunity to harm us or anyone else. We are aware of the risks and the danger, and we understand that we must use force at times to maintain the security of the institution and the safety of the larger society. Unlike many in our society, we are not in denial about violence. Correction officers study and understand force, and we use it, as a tool in our arsenal to maintain control of the inmates.

Key 10

An Inmate's Biggest Problem Is Another Inmate

Most inmates won't attack officers and are not worried about being attacked by officers.

I don't want you to think that everyday you will be fighting for you life. I just want you to be prepared for the unexpected. The truth is, most inmates won't attack officers and are not worried about being attacked by officers. They are worried about being attacked by other inmates. An inmate's biggest problem is another inmate.

An inmate's biggest problem is not you, the officer, because you have rules to follow. An inmate knows that if he is respectful and follows the rules he won't have a problem with you or any other officer. This is not the case when it comes to his fellow inmates. He can be respectful to them and follow all the rules and still be the victim of a brutal attack.

Inmates often attack one another for senseless reasons. I know an inmate who lost his right eye one afternoon because he was singing too loudly while another inmate was trying to sleep. I know an inmate who was slashed from his temple to his mouth by an inmate that he assisted in the law library everyday for a month. One day the inmate he was assisting came into the law library and slashed him, then apologized, and said his gang made him do it. I have met many inmates who were victims of attacks and genuinely had no idea why. And of course there are inmates that attack each other for their possessions all the time. Jail is a tough place for inmates.

Sometimes an inmate may become problematic for you, the officer, because he is afraid of another inmate or a group of inmates. To show them that he is tough he may pick a verbal argument with you. He knows that you have rules concerning when and how you can use force, and he knows just how far to go with you. Usually, an inmate won't come out and tell you he is afraid of the other inmates because he doesn't want to look soft. So, his only alternative is to argue with the one person in the housing area that won't hurt him if he doesn't go too far—you.

He wants the other inmates to see him arguing with you so they will think he is tough or crazy. So, expect him to confront you in front of the other inmates. This is his defense mechanism against the other inmates, and it has very little to do with you. See it for what it is and don't over react. Try to understand the motive behind his actions.

KEY 11

KINDNESS

Kindness can be viewed as a sign of weakness, if you are being kind to inmates that behave badly.

Showing kindness to inmates is not a sign of weakness. Kindness is a sign of humanity, a show of consideration for others. However, kindness can be viewed as a sign of weakness if you are being kind in the hope that the inmates will behave. Kindness should be used as a reward for correct behavior, not to get inmates to behave correctly. After they behave correctly, then they are entitled to any kindness you wish to show them. You can't show kindness to get compliance; you show kindness after the inmate complies.

If an inmate is misbehaving, and you show him kindness, it may appear that you are weak or afraid of the inmate. Once the other inmates see this perceived weakness, many more will misbehave. They will think that the way to get what they want from you is by misbehaving. You don't want to lose control of your area, so don't show kindness to inmates that have bad behavior.

I am not advocating that you deny the misbehaving inmate what he is entitled to by law. You must give him what the law says he is entitled to. However, do not give him any more than he is entitled to. That's why it's important that you study the minimum standards, departmental directives, and institutional orders so you will know what they are suppose to get and not suppose to get.

Even when an inmate is supposed to get something, the time frame in which an inmate is supposed to receive the item or service is usually determined by the officer. So, if the misbehaving inmate asks you to give him a bar of soap or turn off the lights in his cell, make him wait. Don't just jump up and do what he asks. As an officer, you will always have plenty to do, so just be sure to put that inmate's request on the bottom of your list. Do what you are legally obligated to do, just do it when you get ready. He'll get the message.

If your supervisor makes a tour of your area and that misbehaving inmate runs to the supervisor and complains, tell the supervisor that you had some other duties to perform first. If he asks what duties, tell him duties like security inspections, supervising the telephones, supervising the feeding, breaking up an argument, etc. You get the picture. If the supervisor asks you to write a report, just put it all in a report. Don't be scared. If you have to write a report, it will take up even more time so the inmate will have to wait even longer to get what he wants. The bottom line is: you must maintain control of your house. Most supervisors understand that.

Once the inmate corrects his behavior, you should immediately begin treating him the way you treat the other inmates. Bring him back into the fold. Remember, the goal is to get compliance from the inmate, not to punish him indefinitely. Once he exhibits the desired behavior, you must give positive reinforcement to encourage him to continue in his efforts to behave.

As I mentioned when we examined the third layer of resentment, the troublemaker has been mistreated by authority figures since childhood, usually beginning with his parents. Therefore, his distrust of authority is deeply rooted. As the authority figure, you must ensure that you are fair when dealing with this type of inmate. Numerous positive interactions with you will teach him that he can trust the authority.

Tip: When initially entering an area in which I hadn't worked before and where the inmates were unfamiliar to me, I found it better to come in hard and lighten up as the days and weeks go on. I'm not saying to come in and be mean or a tyrant, but just don't be so eager to give the inmates everything they want. Once you observe that the inmates are behaving correctly then you can lighten up a bit.

If you walk in the first day and give away the store by being too lenient, when you have to assert your authority later the inmates will find it hard to accept. It will appear that you have flipped or you are being inconsistent. When you start out hard and then lighten up, you're letting them know straight off that you have the wherewithal and ability to assert your authority. So, if at some later time the inmates start to misbehave and you have to be hard once again, they will not be so rebellious because they already know that being hard is part of your jailing style.

KEY 12

FAMILY

Spend as much time as possible with your family and friends away from your job.

To have a long, successful, and happy career in corrections you must have some kind of support system outside of the job. This support system can be your family, spouse, friends, or neighbors. Being a corrections officer can be very demanding at times and because we spend a lot of hours in the jail setting, we sometimes tend to get our priorities mixed up. The Department of Corrections (DOC) is no substitute for family and friends. Although you may devote anywhere from eight and a half to sixteen hours a day to the DOC, it doesn't make up for quality time with your family and friends. Although you may be making a killing monetarily, working doubles back to back, you must find a way to balance this with your personal life away from the job.

When I started in 1987 mandatory overtime was at an all-time high. There were no limitations or quotas on the amount of overtime you could work like there is now. We often had to work double shifts *(sixteen hours)* on our first, second, and fourth days and on our third day we would have to work at least two and a half hours overtime for some officer who took time due. *(If you are a new correction officer, you will learn about time due when you get to your facility if not before.)* Occasionally even on our third day we would have to work sixteen hours. It was especially tough on me because I didn't have a car for the first year, so I had to take two trains and a bus from Brooklyn to Rikers Island and back. Although conditions are better now for officers, the demanding schedule can still wreak havoc on your personal life.

There are many ways officers choose to deal with the stress that comes with working long hours in a jail and not all are positive. The one thing that I can tell you is to spend as much time as possible with your family and friends. If you have children, try to spend as much time as possible with them and make sure they are well taken care of by members of your support system when you can't be there. If you have a good babysitter or relative that watches your children, spare no expense concerning them. Always let them know how valuable they are in your life and don't ever take them for granted.

Working as a corrections officer I have missed many Christmases, Thanksgivings, birthdays, cookouts, weddings, New Years Eve parties, and family reunions because I had to work. I was lucky because I had a very strong and understanding support system. If I missed a cookout or other family event, members of my support system would call me or I would call them and they would tell me all about it. They would save me a slice of cake or make me a plate to show that they were thinking of me. And I always made it a point to go and get my slice of cake or plate of barbeque chicken, not because I was hungry and needed the food, but because I needed to stay connected, and they also needed me to stay connected.

Once, when I was on a hospital run *(that's when officers take an inmate from jail to a hospital, usually to the emergency room);* the officers *(there were about eight of us from C-95, A.M.K.C.)* were sitting in the Kings County Hospital emergency room. It was about three in the morning, and we were all conversing. One officer, who was known in C-95 for working overtime, was bragging about all the overtime he had been working. He went on about how he worked overtime whenever he could get it. He told us how he would regularly work sixteen hours a day almost everyday, which meant he worked overtime five out of seven days almost every week. He bragged about how he could get any post he wanted on overtime because the captains and tour commanders (ADWs) counted on him to work overtime and really valued his service. He talked about how big his checks were and how he could buy any car he wanted for cash and so on. Being a young, relatively new officer, I must admit that I was in awe and slightly envious of this officer until an older gentleman in his fifties entered in our conversation.

This older gentleman was a civilian patient lying on a stretcher near by, waiting to be seen. He had been listening to our conversation. He sat up and asked the officer,

"Do you have children?"

"Yeah, I have two boys," the officer replied proudly

"How much time do you spend with your boys?" the older gentleman asked.

The officer, now on the defensive shot back, "Oh, I spend a lot of time with my boys."

The older gentleman then asked, "How do you spend a lot of time with your boys when you just said you work sixteen hours a day almost everyday?"

The officer began to try to explain by saying, "Well, whenever I get home, no matter what time it is, I wake them up and spend about an hour with them, and I spend about an hour with them before I go to work,"

The older gentleman then said, "Okay, so that's about two hours a day with your boys, and sixteen or more hours are devoted to corrections."

Our area of the E.R. went silent as we realized how much of himself he had given to the department and how little he had given to his children. In less than one minute this officer went from being a big man, working big hours, and making big money to being a misguided father who had not yet gotten his priorities straight.

Your children are more important than money and cars. Although they may ask for toys and clothes and things that money can provide, all they really need is you. Material things cannot take the place of a loving father or mother. Time passes quickly, and if you're not careful, your children will be grown, and you will have missed out on those special moments that make your child who he or she is. You can never turn back the clock and do it over again. I know many officers who don't really know their children because they worked too much overtime and were never there to see them grow up. Now their children are grown and in many cases it's too late to form that close bond that every parent should have with his or her children.

Yes, the job is demanding, but there will be plenty of occasions when you will have a choice: stay at work and make more money or go home and be with your family. I hope you make the right choice. (Hint: GO HOME)

Personal Relationships

Being a correction officer is just one part of your life. It is a very demanding career, and the only way you can truly be successful at it is by balancing your career and your personal life outside the job. Over the years I have seen officers struggle with their personal relationships. These are a few suggestions that may assist you in this area.

Gentlemen: Beware of females that just want to get with you because you wear a uniform and carry a gun. There may be a jealous, abusive ex-boyfriend in her past that she may be afraid of. She may need you to protect her from him. Now, I'm not saying don't get involved with her for this reason, I'm saying, go into relationships with your eyes wide open. Make sure she wants you for you and not just to be some sort of bodyguard.

Ladies: Some guys can't deal with the fact that their woman carries a gun and/or makes more money than they do. I know many female correction officers whose relationship with their boyfriend or husband was just fine until she became a correction officer.

Some men feel that their manhood is being threatened and their position in the relationship has changed. It would help if the female who has chosen to become a correction officer reassured her significant other that he is still the man in the relationship. If you have a good, strong, loving relationship, and you want to maintain it, talk to your mate about what he may be feeling; let him know that your feelings for him have not changed.

Some men feel that women should not be correction officers and fear for the safety of their mate. If your mate feels this way, reassure him that the training that you received is the best in the nation, and you have the support of your fellow officers and supervisors. Before you are placed in the jail setting, you are thoroughly trained and prepared to handle any given situation.

My experience has shown me that women can be excellent correction officers. Some of the best officers I have ever worked with were females. Most male inmates are not hostile toward female correction officers. If a female uses her natural intuitiveness and combines that with professionalism, she will learn how to defuse incidents more effectively than some male officers can. Any officer's best defense against a potentially abusive inmate is his or her professionalism and knowledge of the job, not his or her ability to fight. *(However, I have seen female officers who fight as well or even better than some men.)*

Working overtime can affect your relationship.
Remember in the correction department overtime is mandatory. Some of you will have mates that will not understand this. Sometimes it is very hard to plan activities outside the job when you work for the corrections department. However, if you have the right person as a mate, he or she will understand and support you most of the time.

KEY 13

COVER YOUR ASS (C.Y.A.) & REPORT WRITING

Always be able to justify your actions. Remember, the job isn't complete until the paperwork is finished.

C.Y.A. is an acronym for **Cover Your Ass**, which means that you should always be able to justify your actions. As a correction officer you are held to a very high standard. From the time you enter the academy and throughout your career you will receive training in many areas such as law, the use of force, and firearms. This training is given to you in part to ensure that you are fully aware of how the department and the law expect you to conduct yourself on and off the job.

As a correction officer you are also a peace officer. You are the holder of the public trust and that trust must not be violated. You must take seriously the power the citizens of your city and state have entrusted to you.

You also have an obligation to provide for your family. Your children depend on you to keep a roof over their heads and food on the table. You must conduct yourself in a lawful manner at all times in order to live up to your family obligations. The term C.Y.A. encompasses these themes.

Before you engage in any questionable behavior you should ask yourself: how am I going to justify my actions? Ask yourself, "Is my behavior justifiable in the eyes of the law, my department, and in the eyes of my family?" If the answer is no, then do not engage in that behavior. That's the best way to **cover your ass** or **C.Y.A.**

If the actions you are about to take are justifiable, then you should confidently take action, secure in the knowledge that your actions are lawful and consistent with the principles that are required and expected of a correction officer. Then afterward, be sure to document your actions by making the proper notifications and filing the necessary reports. This is the way to ensure that you are covered.

So, let's recap, to **C.Y.A.:**

1. Determine if the action you are about to take is justifiable.

2. Once you determine the action is justifiable, then take the appropriate action.

3. Once the action is completed, make the necessary notifications, and file the necessary reports to document your actions. Then you are covered.

I once saw this saying on a sign in a restroom, but it also applies here: *The job isn't done until the paperwork is finished.*

Writing Reports

I would like to emphasize the third point, which includes writing reports. I know some of us don't like the idea of writing reports. Some officers are hesitant to write reports for fear that their own reports may be used against them. They fear that a supervisor or some slick lawyer may twist their words around to mean something that they did not intend. As a result, these officers become reluctant to get involved in uses of force or other incidents for fear that they will have to write reports afterward.

However, inaction is not always an option. Sooner or later we all find ourselves faced with a situation that forces us to take action. And even if you are not personally involved in an incident you may be required to write a report about something you witnessed. If you are concerned that your writing skills may not be up to par, I suggest you do what I did—take a writing course.

During my second year on the job I enrolled in an adult writing course at a local college. I highly recommend this for officers who worry about writing the wrong thing or having their reports misinterpreted. Once I completed the writing course my writing became clear and concise. No longer was I worried about a supervisor or lawyer misinterpreting what I was trying to say. The writing course was one of the best investments in my career that I ever made.

I not only became good at writing my own reports, I was able to help other officers with their reports, as well. I was no longer reluctant to get involved in uses of force or other incidents that I knew would require written reports because I was confident about my writing skills. Instead of staying in the background, I found myself taking the lead when faced with serious situations that required immediate action. I knew that my writing skills would protect me.

Before taking the writing course I made the mistake of thinking that the less I wrote about an incident the better because that would give the reader less information to use against me. The problem with this approach was that I often left out vital information that would have further justified my actions. I was giving the reader a sketchy outline of what occurred that compelled the reader to fill in the blanks himself. This type of vague writing leaves the door open to misinterpretation.

Don't leave it up to the reader to fill in the blanks. Don't assume that the reader will see the incident the way you saw it. Give the reader enough information to understand why you took the action that you did by describing the whole scene in detail.

For example, if you are involved in a use-of-force incident and had to restrain an inmate, don't just write that you grabbed the inmate and held him on the floor with arm locks and body holds. Give the reader some background information. Explain your justification for grabbing the inmate and be sure to make the reader aware of the way the inmate was behaving before you grabbed him.

If the inmate was behaving aggressively and belligerently, be sure to include that information in your report. If the inmate shouted threats and obscenities at you, be explicit and write word for word what the inmate said. If he approached you with his fists clinched and his arm flailing, and you gave the order to stop and back up, but he continued to approach you, include that information. Inform the reader if you took several steps back while continuing to order him to stop, and your back became uncomfortably close to the wall. Mention how you felt cornered and, in that moment, the only option that you had was to grab the inmate. Then describe the great effort it took to bring him to the ground, and apply arm locks and body holds to restrain him until help arrived.

Paint a picture for the reader. It may take two or more pages to explain exactly what transpired. Don't leave anything to chance. You want the reader to say after reading your report, "I would have done the same thing under those circumstances." That's how you justify your actions and C.Y.A. ***(cover your ass.)***

Always be truthful in your reports. If you witness an officer use force against an inmate, and you feel the officer was doing his job to the best of his ability and not acting maliciously, be sure to emphasize that in your report. Also include the conditions under which the officer acted. The officer who you are writing about will also be required to write a report detailing his or her own actions. When both of your reports are read together, the reader should be able to get a full picture of what happened. But under no circumstances do I suggest that you lie in your report.

If after the investigator(s) collect and review all the reports and feel they still don't have a clear picture of what actually happened, they will probably ask you to write an addendum to your initial report. An addendum is an "add on" to your initial report, which means they want you to go into further detail about the incident. They will usually have specific questions for you to answer in your addendum.

If you have concerns that your report or addendum may be misinterpreted, talk to your union delegate or a senior officer about it or have them proofread it before submitting it, if possible. Often when someone else proofreads your report, that individual can catch mistakes or details that you may have missed. *Before you submit any report, it is always a good idea to have someone proofread it, if possible.*

Above all I suggest that you be truthful in every report you submit. If everyone does what they are trained to do, there should be no reason for anyone to lie. Remember, once you sign your report and submit it, it becomes part of a permanent record. You cannot take it back. If at a later date you change your story, it may mean that your first report was false and you may be accused of submitting false documentation which is a serious offense. So, be sure the reports you submit are accurate and truthful.

If you get involved in an incident and your fellow officer or supervisor acts recklessly, maliciously, or unlawfully, do not lie for him or attempt to cover up his actions when writing your report. We are all adults. We have been trained, and we know the difference between right and wrong. Do not jeopardize your career, your livelihood, and your good name for someone who blatantly disregards the law, and the rules and regulations that govern our actions. This type of officer is dangerous, not only to the inmates but to the officers and general public, as well. If you try to cover up for this type of officer, he may destroy your career along with his own. These types of officers give all correction officers a bad name.

It is commendable to be loyal to your fellow officers, but your greatest loyalty should be to yourself, your family, and the law. It's always better to tell the truth in these types of situations and let the chips fall where they may. Maybe that officer's behavior can be corrected or maybe he was not cut out to be a correction officer. Don't jeopardize your career for anyone who acts unlawfully and don't expect anyone to jeopardize his career for you if you act unlawfully. Be professional, responsible, and always cover your ass.

Tip: If you lack confidence in your writing skills or just want to improve them, take a writing course. It worked for me. However, if you don't have time to take a course, you don't have to wait until your next use-of-force incident to practice your writing skills. You can practice and improve your writing skills on your own. A good way to practice writing is by writing about an experience that you enjoyed.

For example, if you went to a party or some other type of event and had a good time, then write about it. It is always easier to write about something that you enjoyed. See if you can put into words what happened and how you felt that day. See how many details you can remember.

Describe the feeling of excitement and anticipation you experienced as you prepared to go to the event. Be sure to describe the happiness you felt when you met up with your family and friends. Don't forget to include what happened on the way home after the event was over. You might want to include approximate times and places.

This type of writing is for your own enjoyment, so you don't have to show it to anyone if you don't want to. However, if you feel confident enough, let someone who also attended the event read it. He can help you remember details that you may have left out. This is a good way to improve your writing skills; with practice your writing will become clear and concise. Once you develop your writing skills, you can apply them to your report writing at work.

Key 14

Don't sleep on Post

It is dangerous and against the rules.

Because jails function twenty-four hours a day, seven days a week, 365 days a year, there will be plenty of nights that you will be working at the jail. Sometimes you will have to work overtime on the 11:00 P.M. to 7:00 A.M. tour or the midnight to 8:00 A.M. tour, and it will not be unusual that you will be sleepy on post. Of course the correct advice to give you is to be sure to be well rested before you go to work, but I know from experience that this is not always possible.

When you are sleepy at work, please try to stay awake. Don't fall asleep around inmates. It is dangerous, and it's against the rules. Walk around, have some coffee, or start a conversation with an officer or an inmate. Maybe take a short nap when you go to meal. After you have worked with the same inmates for a while, you may become comfortable around them. You may even feel comfortable enough to sleep around them, DON'T!

In New York City, correction officers are required to be inside the housing areas with the inmates in most of the jails. If you are assigned to the A post, you will be in the A Station and isolated from the inmates. If you must sleep, this is the best place to do it. However, I am not advising you to sleep there either.

If you're on the B or C posts, you will be inside with inmates. Always stay awake. Even if you are in a cell area, and the inmates are locked in. You must stay awake because inmates have been known to tamper with the locking mechanism on their cell doors. Inmates may be able to get out of their cells.

Why You Shouldn't Sleep on Post

One reason why I never made a habit of sleeping on post was because of an incident that happened to an officer I knew. She was sleeping in the back of a dorm one night on the midnight tour. While she was asleep the inmates took turns masturbating and ejaculating on her face. She woke up with a face full of semen and didn't know which inmates had done it. She couldn't tell her supervisor without admitting that she was sound asleep on post, and even if she did tell the supervisor, she didn't know which inmates had done it. So, the incident never got formally reported. However, it was the talk of the jail for many weeks because the inmates in that housing area told everyone who would listen.

Can you imagine such a thing happening to you? How would you face your fellow officers and the inmates after such an incident? After reading this, you should have all the motivation that you need to stay awake while on duty.

Key 15

Drugs In Jail

How drugs get into jails and the steps that can be taken to prevent this from happening.

Drugs exist in jail. Drugs are brought into jails by visitors. Visitors have been known to hide drugs in books or clothes that they bring to inmates. Check these items thoroughly. Visitors also hide drugs on their persons or on their children. Drugs have even been found in diapers that are worn by infants. When the infant is passed to the inmate, he gets the drugs out of the infant's diaper.

Sometimes a visitor will place a small amount of drugs in small rubber balloons, then smuggle the balloons into the jail in her underwear. At some point during the visit, the visitor transfers a balloon from her underwear and puts it in her mouth. Then the visitor kisses the inmate, transferring the balloon to the inmate during the kiss. The inmate then swallows the balloon. This maneuver is repeated several times. When the inmate gets back to his housing area, he induces vomiting to retrieve the balloons. If he cannot vomit up all the balloons, he will wait until he defecates and then retrieve the remaining balloons from his feces.

If you are assigned to the visit area, watch the inmates and visitors closely. Sometime inmates work in teams; one distracts the officers by faking an argument or asking questions, while the other receives the drugs. Try not to allow yourself to be distracted. If you have a visit search post, search the inmates thoroughly after their visits to prevent drugs from getting into the jail.

These things are basic and most correction officers are very observant and know how to search. That is the best way to limit the amount of drugs that get into the jail. However, searching inmates and visitors does not prevent all drugs from getting into the jail. Unfortunately, officers and other civilian staff *(i.e., cooks, clergy, teachers, nurses, etc.)* also bring drugs and other contraband into the jail. This is very difficult to prevent because it seems that there's always an officer or civilian staff member who feels he is underpaid and sees bringing drugs into jail as an easy way to make additional money.

The way this usually works is an inmate offers to pay an officer or civilian staff member money to bring in drugs. A relative or friend of the inmate meets with the officer at a predetermined location outside of the jail. At that point, the inmate's relative or friend pays the officer and gives him the drugs. The officer then delivers the drugs to the inmate in jail when he returns to work.

Although most jails now have metal detectors and X-ray or line-scan machines at the entrances that officers and civilian staff must pass through, drugs usually are not detected. Officers and civilians are never strip-searched before entering a jail. So, if an officer or staff member carried drugs on his person, he could easily bring them into the jail. I once heard there was an officer that hid drugs in sandwiches and delivered the drugs to an inmate just by handing him a sandwich. It is common for officers to give inmates food in jail, so no one suspected that the sandwiches were lined with packets of cocaine and heroin.

Ironically, these corrupt officers are almost always turned in by the very inmates that they are bringing the drugs. The inmate contacts the DA and tells him he will give him information about a corrupt correction officer in return for a reduced sentence. It works every time. The officer goes to jail, and the inmate gets a lighter sentence or some other agreed upon privilege.

I've worked with two officers who were later arrested for bringing drugs and weapons in to inmates. When I worked with them, I had no idea they were bringing drugs in to the inmates. After they got caught, I began to think about the times I worked with them. The one thing in common that I recalled was that these officers had unusual control over the inmates. The inmates did what ever these officers told them to do without question.

I remember once working in a housing area with an officer named Virgil. Officer Virgil made a comment to the inmates that he needed someone to clean the fan. To my surprise, nearly every inmate in the housing area volunteered to clean the fan. The inmates were almost coming to blows over who would clean the fan. In jail this is highly unusual. You can get inmates to do things like clean fans and mop floors, but they are never happy about it, and they will never ever fight over the privilege to do it.

When I witnessed this behavior I had no idea Officer Virgil was bringing drugs in to inmates. I just thought Virgil was an exceptionally skilled officer. This was early in my career, and I remember hoping that one day I could develop into an officer as skillful as Officer Virgil. Now I know better. If something looks too good to be true, it usually is. The reason the inmates were hanging on his every word and willing to do whatever he told them was because he was bringing drugs in to them.

I witnessed similar inmate behavior when I worked with another officer named Neilson who was later arrested for bringing drugs to inmates. I remember getting into an argument with a group of inmates because I closed their cells. They were accustomed to having their cells open all day. The jail's policy was that inmates receive what is called "options." Every hour during the day and evening tours, the cells were supposed to be opened, and the inmates were given ten to fifteen minutes to retrieve anything they needed from their cells. After ten or fifteen minutes, the cells were supposed to be locked and remain locked until the next hour.

This was not my steady house *(meaning I was not permanently assigned to this housing area)*. Evidently, Officer Neilson didn't enforce this policy. The inmates were very upset with me for closing their cells. They gathered in the corridor and began to loudly protest. Officer Neilson walked over to them and said something that I wasn't able to hear. Immediately, the inmates went quiet and dispersed.

It was unusual that the inmates would just drop the issue the way they did. They obviously were not aware of the policy that I was enforcing and felt they were right to protest against the closing of their cells. How was it possible that Officer Neilson could calm all the inmates down by just saying a few softly spoken words? I didn't hear what he said, but, whatever it was, it worked. I was very impressed. A few months later Officer Neilson was arrested for bringing drugs to the inmates.

There was a third officer who worked in my jail that got arrested for bringing drugs in to the inmates. I had seen him in the locker room and at roll call but had never worked in a housing area with him. So, I can't say what kind of control he had over the inmates. I really became more acquainted with him after he got arrested and sentenced to two years. He was an inmate in my housing area for a brief time. We spoke at length about his downfall, and he admitted that he became greedy. He wanted extra money and thought he would never get caught. The inmate that he was bringing drugs in to made a deal with the DA. When he went to the predetermined location to meet with the inmate's girlfriend, he thought it was just going to be a routine pickup like it was every week. However, this time there were undercover detectives that arrested him as soon as she gave him the drugs and the money.

Please don't assume that every officer that has good rapport with the inmates and can get them to follow his or her orders is corrupt. Officers can achieve this degree of respect from the inmates after a few years of hard work and being firm, fair, and consistent. But trust and respect must be earned; there are no shortcuts.

Be aware, all that glitters is not gold. Watch the officers that you work with and this goes for supervisors and civilian staff as well. Keep your nose clean and don't fall into the trap of bringing contraband in to the inmates.

It usually starts out with an inmate getting an officer to bring in something harmless, like food or candy. The inmate arranges for the officer to receive money for bringing in the items and then this arrangement escalates to drugs, weapons, and other forms of contraband. Don't ever start doing these types of favors for the inmates no matter how much money an inmate or his family offers you. A correction officer who gets arrested and sent to jail has a life behind bars that is twice as hard as the normal inmate. Remember that.

The one thing a drug-dealing inmate loves more than drugs and money is his freedom. If given the opportunity to turn you in to the DA's office in exchange for his freedom, he will do it in a heartbeat. For the DA, drug dealers come a dime a dozen. He would gladly let one or two go for the chance to convict a corrupt correction officer. That would be a real feather in his cap. This point cannot be over emphasized: do not bring drugs and other contraband in to the jails; you will eventually get caught.

Key 16

Always Have An Informant

This section discusses how to establish and cultivate officer/informant relationships with inmates.

An informant is an inmate that gives you information that keeps you abreast of potential problems among the inmates. Informants play an important role in the safety and security of the institution by alerting officers of weapons inmates may have, plots to escape, or plan to start riots or other disturbances. It is wise for you to identify informants and form an officer-informant relationship in which you encourage the inmate to give you information and reward and protect him when he does.

It is always good to establish officer-informant relationships with inmates. However, the best time to establish and cultivate an officer-informant relationship is when an inmate is a *new admission*. A new admission is an inmate who is new to your institution, usually coming off the streets to jail. A new admission can also be an inmate that has been transferred to your jail from another jail.

One of the most dangerous times for an inmate is when he is a new admission because he is not familiar with his surroundings and may not know any of the other inmates. He will go through a period of adjustment before he becomes comfortable in his new surroundings. During this adjustment period the likelihood that he will be attacked by other inmates is at its highest point. He must quickly learn the routine of the jail, which inmates are safe, and which inmates he needs to stay away from. He has to figure out how he fits into his new world. Most inmates feel very vulnerable during this time.

During their adjustment period some inmates deal with the feelings of vulnerability by keeping to themselves and being careful not to offend or cross anyone. While others choose to dive right in and align themselves with a group or gang. The third way an inmate chooses to deal with his feelings of vulnerability is by staying close to the officers. This is the type of inmate you have the best chance of establishing an officer-informant relationship with.

You will notice that this type of inmate will come to you with most of his questions instead of asking the other inmates. He will also position himself in areas that are opposite you, where he can see you, and he knows that you can see him. The reason he positions himself this way is so you can look after him and make sure the other inmates don't attack him. He knows that inmates usually won't perpetrate acts of violence in full view of the officers because they don't want to be caught and sent to punitive segregation or worse, be formally charged by the DA with assault. This type of inmate feels that being in your presence lessens the likelihood that other inmates will attack him.

When the other inmates see you talking to the new admission, they may assume that he is a personal friend of yours or you know him from another jail or housing area. So, they will be reluctant to attack him because they are not sure how you will react. The inmate's feeling of vulnerability is only temporary. This feeling will dissipate as he becomes accustomed to his surroundings and more acquainted with the other inmates. During the period of vulnerability there is a window of opportunity for you to form an officer-informant relationship with the inmate.

While the inmate is in this vulnerable position and indicates through his actions that he needs you to watch his back, play on his need. Act as though you have known him before his admission to your area. Learn and call him by his first name in front of the other inmates and officers. Give him some chores to do in order for him to stay busy and speak up for him by making sure he gets his share of supplies like soap and toothpaste, as well as his share of food. Don't allow the other inmates to exploit his lack of knowledge.

Discreetly school him on what to do and what not to do. Tell him which inmates are safe and which inmates he should avoid. If you need the tables cleaned, call him to you and while you are telling him about the tables tell him about the other inmates as well. The other inmates watching will think you are just giving him instruction on how you want the tables cleaned, but you and he know you are teaching him how to survive in his new environment.

As the days and weeks go by and he becomes more comfortable in his new environment, he will be grateful to you for helping make his transition smooth. Once he has established his place among the inmates begin to discreetly ask him about the other inmates that you suspect may be harboring weapons or receiving contraband. If you feel he has information but is reluctant to tell you, don't hesitate to remind him of how you helped him when he first arrived. Play on his sense of fear by telling him that you need his help to keep the area safe and free of weapons. Make him see the value to his own safety of keeping dangerous prison-made weapons like shanks and shives out of the hands of more violent inmates.

If you feel it is necessary, enlist the assistance of your area supervisor to get information out of the informant. Your informant may be afraid to tell you what he knows because he may believe that the other inmates are watching him. In this case, have your supervisor arrange a confidential meeting with the informant in his office or somewhere else where the other inmates will not see him talking.

If your informant gives you information about another inmate harboring weapons or some other contraband, don't go immediately marching down to that inmate's cell and begin searching. This will alert the other inmates that you are getting inside information, which may put your informant in danger. Your goal is to get information from your informant, not have him exposed and branded as being a snitch.

If you receive important information like the identity of an inmate that has a shank, pass that information on to your area supervisor or security captain who can conduct a search of the entire area. Although the inmate that is reported as having the weapon is the target, when the entire area is searched and the weapon is found, it will appear to be at random. The targeted inmate and the others will not suspect that someone told you about the weapon.

An informant can also give you useful information about plans to attack another inmate or a gang war or riot that is about to break out. If you receive information about a particular inmate that is going to be attacked, your best course of action might be to transfer the targeted inmate out of the area. In the case of two gangs of inmates preparing to fight each other, you and your area supervisor can take steps to transfer and separate the leaders of the gangs and have additional staff on standby to quickly quash any violence before it gets out of hand. Reliable information from an informant can prove to be very valuable in the effort to maintain control of your jail.

It is very important to keep your informant's identity secret. Your informant will only give you reliable information if he is sure the other inmates won't find out. Assure him that whatever he tells you is confidential and the other inmates will never find out. In the event the other inmates begin to suspect that your informant is giving you information it may be wise to transfer him to another housing area or even to another jail. He is no use to you or anyone else if the inmates discover he is an informant. The other inmates will shun him and no longer trust him. He will also be considered a snitch and in real danger of being attacked.

If you have to transfer your informant to another area for his own safety, be sure to tell the officers in his new area that he is your informant, so they can protect him and continue to use him as an informant. In corrections, loyalty is very important. If your informant is loyal to you, then you must also be loyal to him by ensuring his safety and keeping his identity as confidential as possible.

It is much more desirable to cultivate your informants when they are new admissions because they will prove to be more loyal to you than other inmate informants that have already established themselves amongst the other inmates.

You must also be suspicious when a well-established inmate readily offers up information without being asked or with very little prodding. Although good, reliable information can come from any inmate, be aware that an inmate may have selfish motives for giving you information. An inmate may appear to be helpful in providing information but the information he is feeding you may be false. He may try to use you as a tool to harass his enemies. Or he may tell you about an inmate that has a weapon just to disarm that individual so he will be easier to attack. These inmates are double agents with an agenda of their own. They will try to win your confidence and use you to do their dirty work. Keep these inmates at a distance, don't trust them, and don't allow them to use you to attack their rivals.

KEY 17

THERE'S NO SUCH THING AS A FAIR FIGHT

There is no honor among thieves.
Never expect an inmate to fight fair.

Several times in my career inmates have asked me to allow them to have a fair fight with each other. The two inmates had a dispute that they felt could only be settled by having a fistfight. They asked for my consent because they do not want to receive an infraction for fighting which would land them in the Bing. I always said no.

Never consent to inmates fighting because it is against the rules, and I know from experience that there is no such thing as a fair fight in jail. Now, if your jail or prison has a boxing program and a boxing ring, then inmates can settle their differences in a regulated, controlled environment, but absent a boxing program, you should never consent to inmates having a fair fight.

What starts out as a fair fight between two inmates can easily escalate into a fight with weapons like razors, shanks, and knives. While the two inmates are fighting, another inmate can hand one of the fighters a shank, and the fair fight may become a homicide. If you told the inmates that they could fight, then you will be held responsible for whenever injuries are sustained as a result of giving your consent.

Inmates who really want to fight are going to fight whether or not you give them your consent. So, tell them no when the inmates ask if they can have a fair fight. If they chose to fight anyway give each participant an infraction and send them to the Bing[1]. That is the only way you can protect yourself in these types of situations.

An inmate who has a dispute with an officer may ask that officer to have a fair fight with him. An officer should never fall for this type of challenge, even if he knows he could win a fair fight with the inmate. I've said it before, and I will say it again, there is no such thing as a fair fight in jail. There is no honor among thieves. If you consent to fight an inmate, and you begin to get the best of him, another inmate may give him a weapon to use against you or may jump in and attack you, as well.

In corrections, we call five officers against one inmate a fair fight because with five officers the officer will never lose. Our job is not fighting one on one with inmates. If you like fighting and want to match your skills against a single opponent, then become a boxer or a mixed martial arts fighter (MMA fighter). You will make a lot more money that way. We correction officers only fight when it is abso-

[1] *The Bing is a punitive segregation unit in the jail where inmates that violate the rules of the facility are housed. During their stay in the Bing their activities are restricted and they are usually locked in their cells for 23 hours a day.*

lutely necessary, and our goal is to go home from work in the same condition in which we arrived at work— without any injuries. If it takes five officers against one inmate to accomplish that goal, then so be it. So, never forget that in jail there is no such thing as a fair fight.

Key 18

Never Let Them See You Sweat

Maintain a cool, calm demeanor because when some inmates know what upsets you they do that very thing just to aggravate you.

I had a partner who was a good correction officer; however, whenever something bothered him you could see it on his face. His face would become beet red. It was easy to tell what bothered him by just watching his physical reaction. After working with him for a few weeks, I felt comfortable enough to tell him what I had observed. I told him his appearance changed whenever he was upset. He was not aware of it. At first he didn't believe what I was telling him was true. To prove my point I began commenting each time I noticed that he was upset. He finally realized that I was telling him the truth.

When dealing with inmates it's not a good idea to let them know when you are upset. If they know what upsets you, they will do that very thing just to aggravate you. It's good to let them know what you expect from them, but it is not good for them to know what upsets you. You should try to maintain a cool, calm, and collected demeanor. You should have an even temper, never getting too high or too low. Remember, you are a professional; don't let the inmates see you sweat, especially over the small things.

Although I did not like it when the inmates sat on the dayr oom tables, I never became aggravated or upset when they did. I wouldn't yell at them or get angry about it. I would just tell the inmate to get off the table and explain that I did not allow sitting on the tables because it was unsanitary to sit on tables that they would later have to eat off. Had I been upset or aggravated about it, they would have noticed. Seeing me visibly aggravated would have caused the inmates to be more defensive and less compliant.

Once inmates know what really upsets you they will always know how to get under your skin. They will do that very thing whenever they don't get their way, just to upset you. They will use it as a weapon against you. Remember, you are establishing a demeanor that will last your entire career, which may last twenty years or more. Don't make the mistake of getting aggravated over the little things the inmates do. That's a sure way to become burned out. Establish a calm and cool demeanor, and you will be able to deal with inmate behavior much better.

My partner took my advice and changed his reaction to the things that the inmates would do. Instead of becoming flushed, he learned to better control his emotions and stay calm. He began to smile more and see the humor in the way the inmates behaved.

Being able to control your emotions is necessary to control the level of stress you have. By controlling your stress level, you will be less prone to having stress related illnesses. So, never let them see you sweat.

KEY 19

KNOW YOUR INMATES (THE AQUARIUM)

Observe the inmates' individual personalities. It will help you become more effective in foreseeing problems.

In key 3 I talked about troublemakers, how to identify them and how to control their behavior. However, it is not enough just to know how to identify the troublemakers. You will encounter many different types of inmates. The better you know their individual personalities, the more effective you will be in gaining their cooperation and compliance. Jail is a closed environment, sort of like an aquarium. In an aquarium you have different types of fish all living together, and in a jail you have different types of inmates all living together.

If you observe the fish in an aquarium, you will notice that some fish will only swim with others of their same species, while others will swim with any other fish regardless of species. You will also notice that some fish will always swim alone. You will see that some fish are predators, while others are prey. Some swim fast while others swim slowly.

It won't be long before you will be able to tell when a fish is sick by the way he looks and acts. After observing an aquarium for a while you will learn the characteristics of every fish in the tank.

The inmates in your housing area are similar to fish in an aquarium. By observing the inmates you will notice that some inmates only associate with those of the same race or of the same gang, while others will associate and socialize with anyone. You will also notice those inmates that stay to themselves and want to be left alone. You will notice which inmates are the predators and which are the prey. And when an inmate is sick, you will be able to tell right away. Like the fish in an aquarium, you will learn the characteristics and personalities of the inmates in your custody. You accomplish this by interacting with them and observing the way they interact with one another.

If an inmate's behavior has become strange and uncharacteristic that may indicate that he is in need of psychiatric attention. See to it that he receives the appropriate psychiatric attention by sending him to the clinic.

Many inmates feel hopeless and not in control of their lives because of their incarceration. These feelings may lead an inmate to think that suicide is his only way out. One of the most important duties we have is to prevent inmates from committing suicide. In order to prevent suicides from happening, we must know the signs or behaviors.

Some of the common signs that indicate that an inmate may be considering committing suicide are:

- When an inmate that is usually jovial and talkative becomes very quiet and withdrawn.

- If an inmate starts giving away his possessions like his favorite sneakers or jeans as if he won't need them later, even though you know he is not being released from custody anytime in the near future.

- When an inmate's demeanor dramatically changes after returning from court. Often inmates consider committing suicide after being sentenced to longer sentences than they expected.

- When you observe an inmate having an argument with a spouse or significant other over the phone or during a visit. Inmates sometimes commit suicide after a breakup. So, watch them closely after an argument.

In a Brooklyn facility where I once worked, an inmate got into an argument over the telephone with his girlfriend. He slammed the telephone down, went back into the dorm area, and got a sheet off of his bed. He then went into the shower, tied one end of the sheet around the bars and the other end around his neck and hanged himself.

Watch for all of these signs among your inmates. If you think that an inmate may be thinking about committing suicide, go and talk to him. Ask if he is okay. Ask if he is thinking about committing suicide. It is all right to ask that question. You are not putting the idea of suicide in his mind if it is not already there. Sometimes an inmate that is thinking about committing suicide will tell you that he is thinking about it. Sometimes he just needs someone to talk with. If he tells you that he is contemplating suicide, refer him to the jail psychiatrist so he can receive the help that he needs.

Although you may follow all these steps, you may still have an inmate commit suicide on your watch. Inmates don't always show signs before they try to commit suicide. So, if an inmate commits suicide in your assigned area during your tour of duty, don't be too hard on yourself. It happens even to the best officers. An inmate that is truly determined to commit suicide is very hard to stop. Fortunately, many inmates are not sure they really want to go through with suicide and that's the type of inmate that we want to get to before they harm themselves.

Those inmates will usually show signs and can be talked out of it. You have a window of opportunity where you can make a difference. If you are observant and know your inmates, you may be able to save someone's life.

When you make your periodic tours, make sure all your inmates are alive and accounted for, especially at night. Don't just count bodies, count live bodies. Just because an inmate is in his cell doesn't mean that he is alive. Don't assume that the inmate is asleep.

The way you determine that an inmate is alive is by watching his chest rise and fall as he inhales and exhales. If the inmate is lying in a position where you cannot see his chest rise and fall, make some noise by knocking on the cell door or by clearing your throat. This will cause the inmate to stir, and then you will know that he is alive.

If the inmate still doesn't move, then you must take further steps to ensure that the inmate is alive. You may need to go in the cell and shake the inmate. But, before you go into an inmate's cell, alert your partner that you are going into the cell, especially on the night tour. Inmates have been known to set these types of traps for officers.

If you shake the inmate and he wakes up, of course he will initially be upset with you. But that's okay. Knowing that he is alive is the important thing. And when the inmate has time to reflect on it, he will realize that you are concerned about his well-being.

Most inmates who commit suicide do so by hanging themselves with a bed sheet, belt, or shoelace. There are many ways for an inmate to hang himself. A determined inmate can be very creative so you must be determined to prevent them from succeeding.

Inmates have been known to tie one end of a sheet to one side of the bed and the other around the neck, then lie down, and put his body weight off the opposite side of the bed. This causes the sheet to tighten and cut off the oxygen and blood flow to the brain. If you are making a tour and peer into the cell, it will appear that the inmate is just sleeping soundly under the covers. In reality, the inmate is not breathing.

An inmate does not have to have his body suspended in the air to commit suicide. So, don't always expect to see that when you tour your area. An inmate can hang himself by tying one end of a sheet to a cell door handle and the other end around his neck. Then by sitting down on the floor of the cell and letting the weight of his body pull against the sheet, the sheet will tighten around his neck enough to cut off his oxygen. If he is not freed quickly, he will die. Inmates also have been known to tie themselves to a sheet and hang under the bed.

Sometimes an inmate who really does not want to kill himself will try to simulate hanging just to get attention. In suicide prevention courses, this is called a manipulative gesture. Some do this in a misguided attempt to appear insane in order to beat their legal charges or to get a transfer to another housing area.

This type of inmate may tie a sheet or belt around his neck and pretend to be hanging when he knows an officer or other inmate is in the general area. Or he will time the officer's tours and time his manipulative gesture to coincide with the officer's walk down the corridor. When the officer looks into the cell and sees the inmate hanging, it appears that the inmate is actually trying to commit suicide. The officer rushes in and cuts the inmate down. This is what this type of inmate wants.

Although, an inmate may only be pretending to commit suicide to get attention, it is very easy to go too far and actually commit suicide. If the officer does not make his tour at the time the inmate has counted on, the inmate may hang himself before anyone arrives to cut him down.

How can you tell if an inmate's suicide attempt is a true attempt or just a manipulative gesture? The answer is you can't tell. That's for the mental health professionals to determine.

If you see an inmate hanging, and you suspect that it may be a manipulative gesture, do not ignore the inmate and let him hang. Cut him down immediately, notify your supervisor, and refer the inmate to the jail psychiatrist immediately. Any inmate who would fake suicide needs to be evaluated by a mental health professional. Those types of inmates need professional help. And never, ever dare any inmate to commit suicide. Even if you suspect he is using these manipulative gestures to get attention. They may just do it.

If an inmate comes to you and tells you that another inmate is hanging in his cell, take it seriously. Go immediately and investigate. Often another inmate will be the one to alert you when someone is trying to commit suicide. However, always let your partner know that you are going to investigate, just in case it is some sort of a trap. Although we want to save as many lives as we can, we must never neglect our own personal safety when dealing with inmates. Your personal safety is of the utmost importance.

When you make your tours try not to be predictable. Don't make it a habit to tour the housing area every hour on the hour or every thirty minutes because the inmates will pick up your pattern and be able to time when you will be coming down the corridor. If you stagger your tours, the inmates will not be able to predict when you will be coming. This way you will have a better chance of disrupting the plans of an inmate who may be considering committing suicide.

Key 20

Avoid Disgruntled Officers

Associate yourself with officers that have positive attitudes and solve problems. Associating too often with disgruntled officers can soil your image.

To be a good and effective corrections officer you need to be a positive role model for the inmates and your fellow officers. You must maintain a positive attitude and have confidence in the system because you are a vital part of that system. Jail is filled with many inmates who have poor attitudes. Many are hopeless and have a negative self-image, as well as a negative view of the correctional system as a whole.

We officers are constantly exposed to these types of inmates with their negative attitudes, and some officers adopt the same negative attitudes that the inmates have. You will notice, when you're in the locker room or the officers' dining area, officers that have negative attitudes about the way the jail is run but offer little in the way of solutions. They just complain. My dad taught me that if you're not part of the solution, you're part of the problem. Complaining all the time doesn't help, it only hurts. Every problem has a solution, and we as correction officers must look for those solutions and work together to make the system work better.

If you are a new officer, avoid officers who are disgruntled and complain all the time so you don't become infected by their negative thinking. If you're sitting at a table in the officers dining area and the officers at that table are just complaining, maybe you should get up and move to another table. You will notice that these types of officers tend to have poor work habits and poor job performance. These officers have the most problems with their supervisors and the inmates. If you fall in with this group, your fellow officers, supervisors, and inmates may think that you share their negative views. Remember that old saying that birds of a feather flock together.

Associate yourself with officers that have positive attitudes, ones that focus on solving problems, not just complaining about them. If you surround yourself with positive officers and avoid negative, disgruntled officers whenever possible, you will become a positive problem solver. You will be looked up to by your fellow officers, supervisors, and inmates.

Key 21

Lead Like Dorothy (The Wizard of Oz Analogy)

You must convince the inmates that it is in their best interest to follow you.

Do you remember the story of *The Wizard of Oz*? The main character, Dorothy, her dog Toto, and her entire house were swept up by a tornado and crash-landed far away from her Kansas home. She landed in a magical place called Oz. She and her dog were lost and far from home, and to complicate matters, when her house crashed-landed it inadvertently killed the Wicked Witch of the East. Her sister, the Wicked Witch of the West, pledged to avenge her sister's death by killing Dorothy and her dog Toto. She also pledged to take Dorothy's ruby slippers.

All Dorothy wanted to do was get back home to her loving family in Kansas. She learned that the only way she would have a chance of returning home was with the help of the Wizard of Oz. So, she and her dog Toto went on a quest down a yellow brick road to see the Wizard of Oz in the hope that he would be able to help them get back home.

We all remember this classic story from childhood and you must agree that it is a very interesting and compelling story, indeed. However, I would like to submit for your review an analysis of the leadership and management skills that Dorothy exemplified during her quest to see the wizard.

Dorothy was a great leader. She knew she had a perilous task ahead, traveling through unknown lands with a wicked witch out to kill her and her dog. Toto was tough but, this innocent duo was no match for a wicked witch with an army of flying monkeys at her beck and call. So, Dorothy did a smart thing, she enlisted the assistance of the Scarecrow, Tin Man, and Cowardly Lion. She was able to form an alliance with these characters, which proved to be invaluable to her quest to see the wizard.

Dorothy managed her people well. When she met the Scarecrow, it was evident that he was not very smart. She didn't take advantage of his obvious mental deficiency nor did she command the Scarecrow to accompany her. She simply noticed that he needed a brain and reasoned that he may be helped by the wizard. She was able to convince the Scarecrow that it was in his best interest to come with her to see the wizard. She inspired him to follow her in the hope that together they both could achieve their individual goals. She was able to convince the Tin Man and the Cowardly Lion to follow her with the expectation that they would be able to achieve their individual goals and better themselves.

A good correction officer manages his inmates like Dorothy managed the Scarecrow, Tin Man, and Cowardly Lion. You must convince the inmates that it is in their best interest to follow you. You can't do this by yelling at them and constantly threatening them with infractions or other punishment. You get them to follow you and buy into your program by being inspirational.

Speak positively to the inmates and inspire them to do things your way. Once you get them to buy into your program don't stop there, motivate them to better themselves. If they have a drug addiction, encourage them to get drug treatment while they are in jail. If they haven't gotten a high school diploma, motivate them to get their high school equivalency diploma. Encourage them to reconnect with their family and children. If they are religious, encourage them to go to religious services. If they have open court cases, urge them to take an active role in their case by directing them to the law library.

Nearly every inmate gets out of jail or prison at some point, and the better they are prepared for their release, the better chance they will have to not come back to jail. Help them prepare for their release. Inspire and motivate them to be better human beings.

Key 22

Don't Take Sides

Do not give the appearance that you are biased against any individual inmate or any group of inmates.

This chapter applies primarily to inmate fights. When inmates fight, it is important that you, the officer, not take sides. Do not favor one inmate over another. Do not openly root for one inmate to win the fight and don't make comments like, "He's finally getting what he deserves" in front of the inmates, even if the inmate that is losing the fight has been giving you problems for the last two months. Remain professional, and don't just stand by and let an inmate be beaten up; take action to stop the fight.

In order to be effective you must not give the appearance that you are biased against any individual inmate or any group of inmates. You don't want to give them the impression that you will allow or condone certain inmates to be beaten up in your presence. You must take action to prevent injury and to let the inmates know that you are fair.

If the inmates think that it's okay to beat up the inmates that you don't like, they will watch you for cues. Once they determine that you don't like a particular inmate or group of inmates, they will target the inmate or group of inmates for attack. Remain neutral. A correction officer has a duty to take action to prevent all fighting from taking place if possible. If a fight is already in progress, we must take some sort of action to stop the fight.

The way you break up a fight between inmates is also very important. Do not try to break up the fight on your own. There should be at least two officers present when an attempt is made to break up a fight. This is for your personal safety and to ensure that your actions are not perceived as favoring one fighter over the other.

For example: If you try to break up a fight alone, you can only hold one inmate, which gives the other the opportunity to pounce on him while he's tied up with you. If you have another officer with you, both of you can hold one inmate, which will not give either an advantage. If there are more than two inmates fighting, you should wait for enough officers to arrive in the area to safely break up the fight without any officers being injured.

If you are the only officer in the area when a fight breaks out, give verbal commands to the inmates to stop fighting, and then call for backup. Wait until backup arrives before you attempt to break them up. While you are waiting, continue to give verbal commands to stop fighting; watch closely and mentally note who is involved and whether other inmates get involved. Sometimes an inmate who is not involved in the fight will hand a shank or razor to the inmate that is fighting. If someone does hand one of the fighting inmates a weapon, you may be able to identify that inmate.

All the details that you observe will be important when you write your report and issue the infractions to the inmates for fighting.

Don't root for one inmate over another. If you are perceived to be biased by the inmates, it will be more difficult to gain the respect of the inmates in the long run. If you start rooting for one inmate over another, you become part of the problem instead of part of the solution. More inmates will fight in your presence and ultimately the areas where you work will become more dangerous.

Lastly, all fights that you witness must be reported, and the supervisor should serve the appropriate infractions. Give all the details in your reports. If you witness one inmate attack another, then that information should definitely be included in your report. If it is determined that one inmate started the fight and the other was just defending himself, then the inmate who started the fight should be punished, and the other should not be punished. These are decisions that are made after the fight and after a full review of all the facts. So, don't take sides, and you will have a better rapport with the inmates and less fighting in your area.

KEY 23

MAKE ALLIANCES WITH YOUR SUPERVISORS

Don't allow small problems with your supervisor to grow and fester into larger problems that jeopardize your personal safety.

Your immediate supervisor is your lifeline in your time of need. If you are under attack by an inmate or a group of inmates or being held captive by inmates, your supervisor will be vital to your safety and well-being. Your immediate supervisor has a duty to come to your aid. He is required to do everything in his power to ensure that you are safe and out of danger.

From time to time, we all have differences with our supervisors; however, those differences should not cloud the fact that you must work as a team. You must ultimately work together to maintain control of your facility. Your supervisor is not your enemy; your supervisor should be considered your ally.

When you don't have your supervisor's support, you become isolated and once you become isolated you become vulnerable. If you are at odds with your supervisors, inmates pick up on that, and it emboldens them. The inmates become aware of a problem between you and your supervisor by observing the way you interact with him or her and the things that you say about your supervisor when he or she is not around. Don't talk badly about your supervisors with the inmates; remember—the inmates are not your friends.

If the inmates see you arguing or being disrespectful toward your supervisor it sends a signal to the inmates that you don't have your supervisor's full support, and there is a division in the ranks. The inmates will look to exploit this division. They will try to get away with more bad behavior because they know you and your supervisor don't have a good working relationship.

They know that you will be reluctant to call your supervisor for assistance when they act up, and they know that when you do call the supervisor, he may be reluctant to respond promptly. The inmates will also try to turn your supervisor against you and do further harm to your working relationship when the supervisor does respond. They will try to persuade your supervisor that you are at fault, and your supervisor will be more likely to believe the inmates if you and your supervisor are on bad terms.

Don't allow small problems with your supervisor to grow and fester into larger problems that jeopardize your safety and the safety of the institution. The way to stop problems from growing is through communication. Ultimately, you and your supervisor have the same goals. You both want to keep the inmates under control and you both want to remain safe while doing it. Although your methods may be different, your goals are the same. Never lose sight of this fact.

From my experience, I have learned that most supervisors will work with you and support you once they know that you are committed to performing your duties to the best of your ability. They can work with you if you give an honest effort. However, if you're not performing your duties it will be almost impossible to form an alliance with your supervisor.

If your supervisor tours your area, and your logbook is never up to date, you will eventually have a problem with your supervisor. If fights and injuries are occurring in your area, but you have no idea who was fighting or why, you will eventually have a problem with your supervisor. If things like cell doors, light fixtures, or windows are broken, but you did not know it until your supervisor brought it to your attention, that's an indication that you are not performing your security inspections. Most supervisors will have a problem with this. And if the inmates are constantly approaching your supervisor with problems that you should be able to solve, but haven't, then you will eventually have a problem with your supervisor.

Supervisors are prepared to assist you, but they will not do your job for you. They want to see you take the initiative and do as much as you can without their assistance. If you are making an earnest effort to do your job, most supervisors will applaud your efforts and be there promptly when you call for assistance. But if you are a slacker and expect your supervisor to rush to your aid, you may be disappointed.

Be an upstanding officer and get to know your supervisors by speaking with them when they tour your area. If you disagree with your supervisor's instructions, discuss it with him. Most supervisors will take your views into consideration. However, if you don't communicate with your supervisor when you have a different view, he will assume that you are in agreement with him and will expect you to carry out his instructions. When you fail to carry out their instructions, they will view you as a problem.

If you communicate with supervisors and respectfully make them aware of any concerns you may have; they will view you as a thoughtful and conscientious officer. If you perform your duties and are aware of what is going on in your assigned area, your supervisors will respect you and listen to you when you have a difference of opinion or recommendation.

Talk with your supervisors and let them know what type of officer you are by your actions and your words. Let them know that you will not call them for nonsense, but when you do call them for assistance you expect them to promptly respond and take the appropriate action. Your immediate supervisor should be like a knight in shining armor. When you call your supervisor for assistance, you should feel confident that your supervisor will come to your aid and help you solve any problem you have. And your supervisor should be confident that you have done everything in your power before calling for assistance.

This type of confidence in your supervisors, and their confidence in you, can be achieved through communication and working together over time. A working relationship, like any other relationship, is a two-way street. There must be mutual respect between both parties. You must know what your supervisors expect from you and your supervisors must know what you expect from them.

When the inmates observe you and your supervisors positively interacting with each other, it sends a definite message to them. The message being sent is that you and your supervisors are working together. They know if they have a problem with you, they also have a problem with your supervisors, as well. They know you are not working alone. They realize that your supervisors have your back and will promptly respond when you call. They will know that they have very little chance of persuading your supervisors that you are at fault. You have left no division they can exploit. The inmates will be less problematic and more compliant with you because of the alliance between you and your supervisors. It will make your job and your supervisor's job much easier.

When the Supervisor Is at Fault

A supervisor who barks orders at an officer, and degrades and embarrasses him or her in front of the inmates not only makes the officer's job more difficult, but makes his own job more difficult as well. If a supervisor does not respect or trust the officer to do the right thing, the inmates will find it hard to respect and trust the officer as well. The inmates will want to appeal every unfavorable decision the officer makes. The supervisor has created a situation where the officer will call on him more often because the inmates will demand to speak to the supervisor more often.

The supervisor will have to return frequently to the area in order to maintain order because he has usurped the officer's authority by degrading and disrespecting the officer in front of the inmates. In this type of situation, the inmates no longer see the officer as the one who is in control of his area; they see the supervisor as the one who is in control of the area.

If the officers are constantly calling a supervisor, the supervisor is usually at fault. Officers will contact their supervisor more often if they are not sure how their supervisor will react to the decisions that they make. The officers will feel compelled to seek their supervisor's approval before they make a decision. They won't feel confident in their ability because their supervisor has not shown any confidence in them.

The more a supervisor degrades and disrespects his officers, the less confidence the officers will have in their own ability to manage the inmates. This will cause the officers to seek constant guidance from their supervisor. It's a vicious cycle that supervisors create and then these very same supervisors complain about the officers calling them all the time. They fail to realize their role in causing this cycle.

If you are a supervisor and notice that you are receiving many more calls for assistance than your fellow supervisors, take a moment to reflect upon your supervisory patterns. Observe the way your fellow supervisors communicate and interact with their officers. Most likely, you will notice a difference in your approach to supervision. Ask yourself are you empowering your officers or are you trying to micromanage them?

A supervisor must also realize the importance of having a working alliance with the officers he supervises. A supervisor must use his authority to empower the officers and inspire confidence in them. A supervisor should never degrade or embarrass an officer in front of the inmates. Show confidence in your officers, and they will be confident in their own ability to control their inmates. Believe in them, and they will believe in themselves. This will create a better working environment for supervisors and officers.

Abusive Supervisors

In every group you have bad apples and I would be remiss if I didn't let you know that there are supervisors that abuse their authority and take advantage of officers. When you encounter an abusive supervisor be careful and document everything. Start your own personal notebook and write down what he is doing that is abusive or makes you feel uncomfortable.

The best way to deal with an abusive supervisor is to have witnesses to their abusive behavior. If you don't have witnesses don't be discouraged. Abusive supervisors are often careful not to let others witness their abusive behavior. Continue to document the abuse in your personal notebook. Make sure the notes are detailed and in chronological order, complete with the dates and times when the incidents occurred. Take whatever information you have to someone, preferable the union delegate in your facility. They can advise you what to do next. Even if you are on probation you can still bring any problems to your union delegate for advisement.

If your job is not unionized and you do not have a union delegate, you should report the abusive supervisor to his or her supervisor. Go up the chain of command until you get results and document your conversations with each supervisor. You can also report an abusive supervisor to the Internal Affairs Division or to the Inspector General's Office.

Beware of supervisors who will try to get sexual favors from you as blackmail for not writing you up. I have heard stories about a supervisor who would come to new female officer's posts with a duplicate set of keys. He would open the gate with his key while the female officer was not looking, and walk onto her post. He would then tell the officer that she had left the gate open and if he wrote her up she would lose her job because she was on probation. He would then say he would forget the incident ever happened if she would meet him after work. He would then demand sexual favors from the officer as payment for not writing her up.

This is an example of sexual harassment. It doesn't matter if you are male or female, gay or lesbian, you can be the victim of sexual harassment. Sexual harassment is illegal. If you are being harassed, contact your facility's union delegate or contact your facility's Equal Employment Opportunity Commission (EEOC) officer. They are trained to deal with these types of situations. You will not be terminated. Do not believe the supervisor that tells you otherwise.

If you don't have an EEOC officer at your facility or do not feel comfortable talking to the EEOC officer or any of your supervisors, call the U.S. EEOC Office at 1-800-669-4000 and file a formal complaint. Sexual harassment is illegal and has no place in any work place, especially in the law enforcement profession.

KEY 24

RESIST THE URGE TO LET THE INMATES DO YOUR DIRTY WORK

Some inmates will want to get on your good side. Some will go as far as to fight your battles for you.

As you become more and more comfortable with your role of correction officer and you develop your leadership skills, you will notice that some of the inmates will become very helpful. They will want to get on your good side. Some will go as far as to fight your battles for you. Do not allow them to do that.

Once the inmates become accustomed to your routine, they will not want that routine to change. They will become protective of their routine and will view anyone who seeks to disrupt that routine as a threat. They will perceive other inmates that give you problems as a threat to their way of life while in jail.

When an inmate gives you problems, the other inmates may feel compelled to confront that inmate. Some may want to harm the inmate in order to maintain the established routine, while others may want to harm the inmate as a way to endear themselves to you or as a favor to you. Don't let them fight your battles for you.

In these types of situations, it's easy just to sit back and allow them to harm the inmate that is giving you a problem. To an outsider, who doesn't know the politics of your area, it will seem like an ordinary inmate fight. But, you and the inmates in the area will know that the inmate was attacked because he was giving you, the officer, a problem.

Never give the inmates the green light to assault or attack another inmate. When you do this, you become an accomplice or even the ringleader of the act of violence. There are other ways to deal with problematic inmates. Some of the ways have been outlined in previous chapters. Use those ways to control bad behavior or issue the inmate an infraction if his behavior does not improve. By issuing an infraction, you will cause the inmate to be punished in a manner that is consistent with the jail's legal, punitive policy. When you allow inmates to take matters into their own hands and strike out at another inmate, you are going against the jail's established punitive system.

If your supervisors and jail administrators take their duties seriously, you should have all the support you need to deal with bad inmate behavior in a legal and appropriate manner. It becomes challenging when your supervisors and jail administrators do not take bad inmate behavior seriously, and bad inmate behavior is allowed to go unpunished. When bad inmate behavior goes unpunished, problematic inmates become emboldened and the threat to officers' personal safety increases. Under these types of conditions officers feel pressure to allow the other inmates to do their dirty work and punish other inmates for them.

If your jail is truly dysfunctional, and you need the inmates to protect you from another inmate, you should consider transferring out of that facility or resigning from corrections altogether. In this case, the environment is too dangerous. No good can come out of allowing the inmates to do your dirty work.

If the inmates sense that you are dependent on them for your own personal safety, they will begin to pressure you to give them special privileges or pressure you to break the rules for them. This slippery slope can result in the inmates controlling you, instead of you controlling them. Do not allow this to happen. Use every legal means at your disposal to deal with problematic inmates.

Speak to your supervisors about it, and if you don't get results, go up the chain of command, even if you have to go all the way to the warden. If that course of action fails, then you are most likely working in a dysfunctional, dangerous jail. You should consider leaving that jail if possible or resigning from the job.

If you anticipate that you will have a physical altercation with an inmate and there is time to notify your supervisor, then do so and get the appropriate support. If there is not time to notify your supervisor before a physical altercation, remember you have the absolute right to defend yourself. Do not hesitate to defend yourself if you honestly feel you have no other alternative and your personal safety is in jeopardy.

We want to use peer pressure to compel inmates to behave, but there is a difference between using peer pressure and giving inmates the permission or latitude to use violence. Sometimes inmates will genuinely feel loyal to an officer and will feel obligated to protect an officer from harm. However, the officer must realize that it is not proper. Resist the urge to let the inmates do your dirty work.

Key 25

Don't be Too Eager to Please

You have an obligation to evaluate the orders that you are given by your supervisor(s) and determine whether they are proper and lawful.

The best way I can explain what is meant by not being too eager to please is by telling you a story about an officer I use to know.

The Story of Officer Zeus

Officer Zeus was a strong, six-foot-three, two-hundred and-fifty-pound weightlifter. He was in my academy class, and he was far and above the strongest and most athletic recruit in the entire class of over two hundred and fifty recruits. Our physical training instructors often remarked that Zeus was the best recruit they had seen at the academy in years. Upon completion of our academy training, Officer Zeus and I were assigned to the same jail on Riker's Island.

One day during count time, Officer Zeus instructed the inmates to stand by their beds to be counted. One inmate ignored Zeus's instructions and stayed in the dayroom reading a magazine. Officer Zeus went into the dayroom and ordered the inmate to go stand by his bed for the count. The inmate refused to leave the dayroom, and he and Officer Zeus began to argue. One thing led to another, and a fight ensued.

The inmate was no match for Officer Zeus who easily defeated him. Three other inmates, seeing their fellow inmate losing the fight, jumped in and joined the fight. However, the four inmates were no match for Zeus; he was able to single-handedly beat all four of the inmates into submission. By the time the riot squad arrived, Officer Zeus had the entire situation under control.

Rumors of the fight quickly began to circulate throughout the jail. As the weeks went on, Officer Zeus was involved in two more fights with inmates and each time he emerged victorious. Officer Zeus became the talk of the jail among the officers and inmates. In the weeks that followed, the stories of Officer Zeus's fights were told and retold. Many officers began to look up to Officer Zeus as sort of a hero. The inmates had flagged him as someone to look out for and beware. He was on a fast track to becoming a jailhouse legend after only a few months of working in the jail.

The officers and inmates were not the only ones talking about Officer Zeus, the supervisors were talking about him, as well. Many of them felt that Officer Zeus's popularity was a good thing, and the jail needed officers like Zeus to get tough with the inmates. Many also felt that Officer Zeus's popularity provided a needed boost to the morale of the officers in the jail.

The supervisors wanted to use Officer Zeus's notoriety to their advantage, so they began changing his post to areas like the Receiving Room or Movement Control, where he would be one of the officers first to respond to any alarm throughout the jail. He would often be assigned to the probe team, an assignment that was usually given to officers that had several years of experience. This was very unusual because Officer Zeus was getting these preferred assignments with only a few months' experience as a correction officer.

Officer Zeus felt good about all the attention he was getting, it made him feel important and special. In the months that followed, Officer Zeus responded to many alarms and battled with dozens of inmates. His supervisors encouraged him to be aggressive with the inmates, and they often praised his actions at the officers' roll calls.

Zeus felt like he was on top of the world. He thought that he had finally found his niche, the one thing that he was good at. He was proud that in less than a year he had made a name for himself.

Three days before he was scheduled to complete his probationary period, Officer Zeus was terminated. They told him he was being terminated because he had too many uses of force.

Many officers mistakenly believe that their job is secure if their immediate supervisors are happy with their job performance. This is not always the case. The law gives you the authority to act as a correction officer. You have an obligation to evaluate the orders that you are given by your supervisor(s) and determine whether they are proper and lawful. If you are given an order that is unlawful, you are not required to carry out that order.

Furthermore, you must ensure that your actions are not detrimental to your own career. Do not allow yourself to be used by anyone and do not become a puppet of your supervisors. Make sure your actions are within the law and consistent with the lawful policies of your department.

If you are being called on to engage in uses of force, while other officers are not being called on, ask yourself why. Corrections is a team effort so, don't be reluctant to question your supervisors as to why you are being called on while your fellow officers are not, especially while you're on probation. While you are on probation be careful not to get involved in an inordinate number of incidents, if you can avoid them. Sometimes it may be necessary to remind your supervisors that you are still on probation and make them aware of the amount of incidents that you have been involved in. They may not know.

When you are evaluated at the end of your probationary period, you do not want to have twice as many incidents as your fellow officers that are also having their probationary evaluations. Your immediate supervisors may not be on the committee that is performing your evaluation. The committee members probably will not know you personally. They may not know that you are a great officer.

All they see is a file with your name on it. If that file has thirty use-of-force incidents, while every other officer's file in your group has an average of four use-of-force incidents, you may appear to be more prone to use force than your coworkers. You may be seen as being more violent than the average officer, which in their opinion may prove to be a legal liability to the department in the future.

The academy class that Officer Zeus and I were a part of had 254 recruits. Assuming that most of us made it to the end of our probation, there may have been well over 200 of us having our last probationary evaluations at the same time. The committee charged with determining who would pass or fail their probation most likely did not know us personally and only used our service records to evaluate us.

When the committee saw Officer Zeus's file come across their desks, with the records of his involvement in dozens of uses of force, and compared that to the average recruit that was involved in only four uses of force, Zeus probably stood out like a sore thumb. They probably assumed that Zeus was a hot head or quick tempered. They probably decided that it was better to terminate Officer Zeus rather than keep him and have to defend him and his record in a lawsuit in the future. The committee had no way of knowing that the supervisors were calling on him to engage in these uses of force. His supervisors still have their jobs, but Zeus was terminated.

The same goes for other areas of job performance like your attendance. If you have twice as many absences than the average officer who is also having his final probationary evaluation, you may be seen as a future problem. They may conclude that you will be calling in sick more than the average officer will throughout your career. They may terminate you for this reason. Keep all absences at a minimum throughout your career, especially while you are on probation.

While you are on probation, you are supposed to be learning the job and observing the seasoned, experienced officers. It is best for officers that are on probation to keep a modest profile, if possible, and allow the more experienced officers to take the lead when dealing with potentially volatile situations.

KEY 26

DON'T PROTECT THE INMATES TO YOUR OWN DEMISE

Understand how your fellow officers and supervisors may interpret your actions.

Your position as a correction officer requires you to be loyal to your fellow officers. In addition, your position as a correction officer also requires you to protect the inmates from harm. So, if you believe your fellow officer is harming an inmate, what should you do? Should you support the officer? Should you help the inmate? Or, should you stay neutral? Of course, you want to do what is right, however, sometimes knowing what is right can be difficult. Sometimes there is no right answer. Sometimes, whatever choice you make could end up being the wrong choice.

There are gray areas that officers, who want to do the right thing, should be aware of. The best way to illustrate this gray area is by giving you the following example of what happened to an officer named David Moore.

David was another one of my academy classmates. He was very popular while he was in the academy because he had a very nice personality combined with a great sense of humor. Whenever we were feeling down, David would make a witty remark or tell us a funny joke to lift our morale.

After we graduated from the academy, David was assigned to ADRC, the adolescent facility on Rikers Island. One day, an officer he was working with, named James Wilson, got into a fight with one of the inmates. David responded to the area and saw that Officer Wilson was getting the best of the adolescent inmate. At that point, David attempted to break up the fight by grabbing and holding Wilson. During the commotion, while David held Wilson, the inmate produced a razor and slashed Officer Wilson across the forearm. David pressed his body alarm, and the response team responded, recovered the razor, and removed the inmate from the area. Officer Wilson was rushed to the hospital where he received several stitches to close the gash in his forearm.

Officer Wilson eventually recovered from his wounds and came back to work. However, David's career in corrections was in great peril because of this incident. Although he had no way of knowing that the inmate Officer Wilson was fighting had a razor, the officers and supervisors who worked at his jail blamed him for Officer Wilson's injuries. They viewed David as an "inmate lover" or an officer who is more concerned with the well-being of the inmates than the well-being of his fellow officers.

Officer Wilson had been working in the jail for several years and was very well liked by his fellow officers and supervisors. David, on the other hand, had just arrived at the jail two months before the incident and had not established a reputation. Most of the officers who worked at his jail didn't know who David Moore was before Officer Wilson's slashing, but afterward they came to know David and viewed him as a traitor. It was their view that Officer Wilson had been working in the jail for years and had never been injured until he worked with David Moore. They felt that David did not protect Officer Wilson and was the reason why he was slashed. There was nothing David could say or do to change the officer's and supervisor's opinion of him. He tried many times to explain that he didn't know the inmate had a razor, but his explanations fell on deaf ears.

None of the officers wanted to work with him after the Wilson incident. When officers were assigned to work with him, they would loudly protest to their supervisors. The supervisors would often side with the complaining officers because they, too, felt that David was responsible for Officer Wilson's injury.

David was permanently assigned to security posts, where he worked alone. Often when he arrived at work, he would find that his locker had been moved, and he would have to search the entire locker room to find it. He often found it in the shower.

He got little sympathy from his supervisors when he complained. And when he asked for a transfer to another jail, his request was denied, partly because he only had a few months on the job and there was a long waiting list of officers who had requested transfers before him and partly because no other jail wanted to accept him because of the Wilson incident.

So, David put up with the insults and disrespect from

the officers and supervisors until he couldn't take it anymore. Shortly afterward, David Moore resigned from the job. That was a sad day. I knew that David was a great guy and was only trying to do the right thing when he broke up the fight between Officer Wilson and that inmate. If given a second chance David could have proven himself to be a fine correction officer. But he never got that second chance. His jail wouldn't forgive him. They left him little choice but to resign.

I tried to talk him out of leaving to no avail. He knew that it was impossible to work in a jail where you have no support from your fellow officers or supervisors. It's too stressful and too dangerous.

I don't know what David could have done to avoid his fate. Should he have just stood back and watched Officer Wilson beat up the inmate without trying to stop it? I don't know. I wasn't there and neither were you.

Sometimes officers do get carried away and go way past the point where physical force is justified. Sometimes officers use excessive force on inmates that results in serious injury or death. Maybe David was trying to stop what he perceived as excessive force. Maybe he should have waited for other officers to arrive before breaking up the fight, so someone would be present to hold the inmate as well. Maybe David should have watched the inmate more closely while grabbing Officer Wilson to ensure the inmate didn't attack Officer Wilson. Maybe the inmate didn't have a razor when David grabbed Officer Wilson but was slipped a razor by an inmate that was in the crowd.

We can always play Monday morning quarterback and say what we would have done or what David should have done. That's not a bad thing; we should evaluate incidents like these and try to decide what would have been the best course of action because we may find ourselves in the very same position one day. David was relatively new to the job; maybe he wanted to protect the inmate and didn't know the type of inmates we deal with. Some inmates will slash an officer with a razor if given the chance. There is no such thing as a fair fight in jail, and sometimes you have to make very tough decisions in a split second.

Always remember that you are an officer, and you have a duty and obligation to protect your fellow officers. Your fellow officers have that same duty and obligation to protect you. When you are faced with the choice of protecting the officer or protecting the inmate, always choose to protect the officer. If, as in David's case, you are faced with an incident where the officer has the upper hand and may be using excessive force, intervene if you can but be sure that it is safe for you and your fellow officer to do so.

KEY 27

DON'T PROTECT ANOTHER OFFICER TO YOUR OWN DETRIMENT

(MISPLACED LOYALTY)

You cannot protect another officer or remain loyal to him if doing so causes you to violate the very principles that you are sworn to uphold.

Loyalty to your fellow officers is a good thing; however, sometimes loyalty can be misplaced. When an officer places loyalty above the oath to uphold the law, the officer embarks down a path that is not the way of a corrections officer. A corrections officer must stay within the law. You cannot protect another officer or remain loyal to him if doing so causes you to violate the very principles that you are sworn to uphold.

When an officer strays outside the law, he loses the protection of the law and the line between officer and inmate begins to blur. The following is an example of how misplaced loyalty, combined with inexperience, caused the downfall of three well-meaning officers.

Caroline Woods was a single mother who decided to become a correction officer to provide for her three-year-old daughter. She was determined to make the most of her opportunity in the hopes that she would be able to have a career in corrections. So, she studied hard during the academy and after successfully completing her academy training, she was assigned to a jail.

After several weeks at her new jail, an inmate named Joseph Pearson began to give her problems. Each day inmate Pearson would make very inappropriate remarks to her. At first, Officer Woods just ignored him, but day after day, his comments became more frequent and more sexual in nature. He began making comments to her about her body and gave graphic details of what he wanted to do to her.

This made her extremely uncomfortable. Inmate Pearson noticed that his comments made Woods uncomfortable. He began to take pleasure in the young officer's discomfort and became more and more graphic in his comments. On several occasions, he exposed himself to her and threatened her that if she told anyone, he would get violent with her.

Caroline Woods wanted more than anything to have a successful career in corrections so she could provide for herself and her young daughter. She knew that being a correction officer would make her more independent. She was saving her money and knew it wouldn't be long before she would be able to move out of her mother's basement apartment and get a place of her own. She would be able to give her daughter a better life than she had growing up.

Caroline's mother was very proud of her daughter and admired the way she had picked herself up after her daughter's father abandoned them. Caroline was very grateful to her mother for taking them in, even though her small basement apartment had barely enough room for one person, not to mention three. She knew her mother was proud of her for taking the job of correction officer, and Caroline didn't want to let her down.

But, Caroline felt that if her fellow officers and supervisors found out that she was being harassed by Pearson, they would conclude that she didn't have what it takes to be a correction officer. She thought that if they found out that she could not handle this one inmate, she would lose her job. So, she convinced herself that she couldn't tell anyone that she was being harassed, and continued to put up with Pearson's sexual advances and tried to avoid him whenever she could.

This problem began to weigh heavily on her mind. She often could not sleep at night because she was preoccupied with thoughts about what inmate Pearson would say or do to her next. One evening, while she sat in the officers' dinning area on her break, three male officers she knew from the academy came in to the dinning area. They had not seen Caroline since they all graduated from the academy because they were assigned to a different area of this very large jail.

When they saw her, they noticed that she didn't look like herself. They remembered her as being a very well-kept and alert woman, but now she looked tired and run-down. Her hair was unkempt and her uniform was wrinkled. They knew this was not the Caroline Woods they remembered from the academy. They sensed that something was wrong. They asked her if everything was all right. At first, she told them that everything was fine, but she could see that they did not believe her. She knew that these academy classmates were her friends and were genuinely concerned about her, so she confided in them.

She told them what she had been going through with this one inmate named Joseph Pearson. She felt relieved that she could finally tell someone about what was happening to her. She knew that they would not judge her or feel that she was at fault.

The three officers listened attentively as she relayed to them the graphic details of what she had been enduring over the last several weeks. They became upset at the thought that an inmate would say such things, expose himself and harass such a nice young woman like Caroline Woods. They were determined not to let this inmate get away with this harassment for another minute. They asked Woods where inmate Pearson was, and she told them that he was in her housing area.

Her three classmates decided to go back to her housing area with her after her break. When they got there, Officer Woods pointed out the inmate that had been giving her so much grief. When she pointed out Joseph Pearson, her three academy classmates went into the housing area and escorted Pearson out into the corridor.

At first inmate Pearson had no idea why he was being led out of the housing area by these three officers, but when one of them asked him why he was harassing Officer Woods, he knew he was in deep trouble. He became afraid because he could see that these officers were not there to talk. He began to stutter and look around to see if anyone else was in the corridor that might be able to help him, but he was out of luck. He was completely alone with these three officers. At that moment, one of the officers punched him hard in the jaw and as Officer Woods watched through the Plexiglas panel of the housing area door, the three officers punched and kicked Pearson repeatedly. Although Officer Woods winced as the officers beat Pearson, she felt that he was finally getting what he deserved. After the three officers beat inmate Pearson to their satisfaction, they dragged him back into the housing area and left him there all bruised, bloodied, and semiconscious.

After the incident Pearson was taken to the hospital and a full investigation was conducted. C.O. Woods told the investigators the whole story including the names of the three officers responsible for the beating. The investigation uncovered that inmate Pearson was harassing Officer Woods, however, the actions that were taken by Woods's classmates were deemed excessive. The three classmates were all still on probation and were terminated for excessive use of force. Officer Woods did not participate in the beating and told the truth when she was questioned, so she was allowed to keep her job and no charges were filed against her.

Although Woods kept her job, the years following this incident were very difficult for her. Many officers and supervisors gave her the cold shoulder because they felt that Officer Woods was responsible for getting her three classmates fired.

Officer Woods and her three classmates were new officers and didn't know what to do when faced with a difficult situation like the one that inmate Pearson created. Officer Woods should have told her supervisor about Pearson's harassing behavior when it first began. She mistakenly felt that if she told her supervisor about Pearson's behavior, it would be construed by her supervisor that she was somehow at fault. This is not true.

If you have a problem with an inmate that you cannot handle you should always let your supervisor know. That is why they are there. They understand that being a correction officer is not an individual activity; it takes a team effort to control the inmates. Every officer needs assistance when dealing with inmates from time to time. There is no shame in requesting assistance from your supervisors or fellow officers.

Supervisors and senior officers expect new officers to ask questions and ask for their assistance when dealing with problematic inmates. Most likely, in Officer Woods's case, the supervisor would have given inmate Pearson an infraction, which would have landed him in punitive segregation (the Bing) for thirty days. Pearson would have been removed from Officer Woods' area, and his behavior would have been properly documented, which would make it easier to send him back to the Bing if he tried to harass anyone else.

Officer Woods and her three classmates made the same mistake—they failed to make their supervisors aware that there was a problem. When Officer Woods confided to her classmates about how inmate Pearson was treating her, the three classmates should have gone to their supervisor with the problem instead of taking matters into their own hands. Although they were just trying to help a fellow officer, they went about it the wrong way.

KEY 28

DON'T WAGE YOUR OWN PERSONAL WAR WITH THE INMATES

It takes a team effort to maintain control of a jail. Officers, Supervisors and Administrators must all work together.

In the previous chapter, the three unfortunate officers who lost their jobs made the mistake that many officers make. They were reacting to the frustration that every officer feels from time to time. The frustration is fueled by the belief that the inmates are getting away with too much. They feel that action must be taken to put the jail back in order. Sometimes groups of officers who are frustrated with the way the jail is being run will form alliances with one another and take matters into their own hands.

The message I have for these officers is that jails and prisons go through cycles. They go from one extreme to another. A jail will have periods when it is run in a very lax way, and inmates will appear to get away with a lot of bad behavior. There are also periods when a jail is run very strictly, and inmates are harshly punished for minor infractions. These two extremes are symptoms of a systemic problem. It is primarily a result of the policies of the warden or the administrators of the jail and not the result of the actions or inactions of the officers.

A jail that is extremely lax is usually the result of a lack of leadership at the top. Lack of proper funding and over-crowding can also cause a breakdown in the proper functioning of a jail. The rules and institutional orders that govern how a jail functions are designed for a set number of inmates. Once the inmate population exceeds that set number, the rules and institutional orders that govern that jail no longer function effectively.

If a jail is designed to hold 1,000 inmates, and the inmate population grows to 1,500 inmates, the original rules and orders that were designed to control 1,000 inmates become less effective. The problem is compounded when the funding for supplies, services, and staffing does not increase with the increase in the inmate population. The administrators of the jail must revise the rules, and increase staffing and services in proportion with the increases in the inmate population for the jail to function properly.

A small band of determined officers cannot solve the problems that come from a lack of leadership and a lack of funding. The officers' determination must be matched with the administrators' commitment to providing the necessary resources to reclaim greater control of the jail. The degree of commitment the administrators have to providing what is needed will have a direct effect on the degree of control the rank and file officers and supervisors have over the inmate population.

When groups of officers attempt to take the jail back from the inmates, without the knowledge or consent of the jail administrators, the group of officers usually becomes the subject of disciplinary action. They often get suspended or terminated, just like the three classmates in the previous chapter. It is a noble effort but usually unsuccessful.

During the lax period, inmates often attack officers, and in retaliation, officers brutalize inmates. It becomes a war of attrition. One day an officer gets hurt, and the next day an inmate gets hurt. During this period, the inmates feel that they can get away with anything. They think that they are running the jail, and the officers are afraid of them. They don't think this period will ever come to an end. That's where they are wrong!

I know that this is a very frustrating period for officers because you are the ones on the front lines. You are the ones being injured. You may feel that the administrators are not aware of what's going on or that they don't care about the officers enough to put a stop to the attacks. During these periods the administrators are like the proverbial sleeping giant.

Most of the time the administrators are fully aware of what is going on but lack the manpower or funding to take action. They may also be still working out the strategy, tactics, and new rules and institutional orders that will be used to put the jail back in order. Administrators also must be concerned with the legality of their strategy and also must gain the approval from their superiors before the appropriate action can be taken. This can take time, but rest assured that the day will come when the sleeping giant will be awakened and all inmates that try to oppose the giant will be swept away.

Afterward, there will be a long period of peace and balance that will permeate the jail, and the inmates will know that the officers are fully in charge. However, inevitably this peace and balance will eventually erode, the giant will go back to sleep, and the inmates will be allowed to get away with bad behavior once again. It is a cycle, and if your career is long enough, you will see this cycle play out several times in your jail.

My advice to the frustrated officers assigned to jails that are currently going through a lax period is to hold on. Don't try to right things on your own. Continue to protect yourselves and your fellow officers. Stay within the rules and wait for the time when the giant awakens.

When that time comes don't go soft and start feeling sorry for the inmates. Stay strong and do what the administrators request that you do. This is the time to set things right. So, don't complain when you have to suit up in riot gear and go to battle. This is sometimes necessary to take the jail back. However, don't use excessive force and don't violate the law or your oath as a peace officer. Afterward, enjoy the long period of peace that will be a result of taking back the jail.

KEY 29

DON'T ANTAGONIZE THE INMATE(S) WHEN THINGS ARE GOING YOUR WAY

Stay professional. Antagonizing an inmate when things are going your way is like throwing gasoline on a fire.

Inmates are under a tremendous amount of stress. Many are facing or serving long prison sentences. For some being incarcerated has turned their lives upside down. Some have lost their jobs, homes, and spouses while they've been locked up. Under those types of pressures, the average person would be stressed out.

Inmates sometimes take out their frustrations on themselves or other inmates. Sometimes inmates will take their frustrations out on the officers. They usually won't physically attack officers, but they will talk back to officers. When you give an inmate an order, and the inmate starts talking back, you should ask yourself whether or not the inmate is complying with your instructions. If he is complying, then there is no real reason to engage in an argument or antagonize him.

For example: If you tell an inmate to go into his cell, and he begins to complain but is walking toward his cell, it is not necessary to respond to what the inmate is saying. The goal is to get the inmate to comply not to argue with the inmate. If he is walking toward his cell that means things are going your way. There is no reason to push the issue. When he enters his cell that means the inmate has done what you wanted him to do.

Sometimes, when you respond to the complaints or ramblings of a stressed out, unhappy inmate you are in effect adding gasoline to a fire. If things are going your way there is no reason to do this. Sometimes meaningless arguments escalate into violent incidents that cause officers and inmates to be badly hurt. One time in particular comes to mind.

On that day, my partner, Officer Citron, and I were doing a meal relief in a housing unit. It was count time, so we told the inmates they had to lock in. All the inmates complied except for one, who just stood in the corridor. When Officer Citron told him to lock in, the inmate began yelling and screaming. He said he was tired of people telling him what to do and threatened to kick Citron's ass if he didn't leave him alone.

Officer Citron did not argue with him, he just told him again that it was time to lock in. But, the inmate refused to lock in and continued to threaten Officer Citron. Although, I was standing right next to my partner, the inmate never directed his comments toward me, he was totally fixated on Officer Citron. It was obvious to Citron and I that the inmate was behaving irrationally.

Once I realized that the inmate was not directing any of his threats toward me, I stepped in front of Officer Citron and began telling the inmate to calm down. At that moment, a captain and three officers were passing by the housing area and heard the inmate yelling and threatening Officer Citron. The captain and the three officers knocked on the housing unit's door, and I opened the door and let them in.

In most cases, the sight of a captain and the three additional officers would cause an inmate to calm down a bit; however, on this day it had no effect. The inmate continued to yell and threaten Officer Citron. At this point one of the officers that came in with the captain began talking to the inmate. He calmly explained that no one was going to hurt him, and we just wanted him to lock in while we took the routine institutional count.

The officer was eventually able to get the inmate to calm down. A few minutes later the officer was able to get the inmate to walk toward his cell. The inmate was still visibly upset and continued to mumble obscenities as he walked slowly down the corridor with the officer. We were all relieved that the officer was able to get through to the inmate. We remained quiet as he escorted the inmate to his cell.

When the officer and the inmate were about two feet from the cell door, the captain said, "See, I knew he wasn't gonna do anything. He's all talk."

He said it just loud enough for the inmate to hear. Once he heard what the captain said, the inmate came charging back up the corridor in the direction of my partner. As he charged up the corridor, one of the officers that had come in with the captain jumped in front of Officer Citron to head off the inmate's attack. The charging inmate punched the officer in the face. The officer that was punched wore glasses and when the punch landed the glasses broke and the frame cut the officer's face.

Then we all wrestled the inmate to the ground. In the process, we broke the inmate's nose and gave him a black eye. Both the inmate and the officer were taken to the hospital for emergency medical treatment.

The injuries to the officer and the inmate may have been avoided if the captain had not said anything. We knew that this inmate was disturbed, agitated, and extremely volatile. The captain's remarks were the equivalent of pouring gasoline on a fire. When the inmate heard what the captain said, he exploded, which caused an officer to sustain a cut to his face. The officer probably bears that scar to this day.

It is not a good idea to antagonize inmates especially when things are going your way. If the inmate is complying or retreating, let him do so without antagonizing him further. Don't add fuel to the fire.

Key 30

If You Can't Reach the Inmate, Let Someone Else Try

Each officer has his own style and his own unique way of dealing with inmates.

In the example given in the previous section, we observed that the inmate's anger was focused on only one officer and not on the other officers present. This will often happen. An inmate, for what ever reason, will have a problem with one officer and not another. This is usually a temporary state of mind for the inmate. Usually, after the incident is resolved, the tension or animosity the inmate has for that particular officer will fade.

When you observe that an inmate is hostile toward one officer in particular it is very important that the other officers present shield the officer that is the subject of the inmate's hostility. It is a good idea to keep that officer away from the inmate as well. Another officer should try talking to the inmate. Just because an inmate is angry with one officer or will not respond to one officer's instructions does not mean he will not respond to someone else. Each officer has his own style and his own unique way of dealing with inmates. If you can't reach the inmate, let someone else try.

In this way many uses of force can be avoided. Don't let your ego get in the way of good problem-solving techniques. Above all, always work as a team and protect one another.

KEY 31

IF YOU CREATE A PLAN, STICK TO THE PLAN

Don't be impatient. Give the plan a chance to work.

Whenever you have an anticipated use of force *(meaning you know ahead of time that you are going to have to use force on an inmate)*, the captain or supervisor should have a plan of how the force is to be executed. Before the supervisor enters the area where the force will be used, he or she should relay to the officers where they should position themselves and what they are supposed to do when the order is given.

For example: If one inmate is to be extracted or moved from an area, the supervisor may have four officers execute the extraction. One officer will usually be responsible for controlling the inmate's right arm, another officer will be responsible for controlling the left hand, the third officer will control the left leg and the fourth officer will control the inmate's right leg. The other officers are instructed to secure the area and prevent any other inmates from getting involved in the extraction. The supervisor should have a code word or phrase that he will say that will set the plan in motion.

If the extraction is executed correctly and the inmate doesn't put up too much resistance, the inmate will not be injured. Neither will the officers executing the extraction. The extraction will go quickly and smoothly. The problem arises when a supervisor and several officers in riot gear enter an area with a defined goal but without a defined plan to achieve their goal.

If the supervisor and officers do not have a prepared plan of action, a routine extraction can turn into an all out battle between the officers and the inmates. Even if you have a plan, there is still no guarantee that everything will go as planned. However, you increase the odds of things going your way if you have a plan.

Once you have a plan you must stick to the plan. Trust your supervisor and your fellow officers. Stay focused and don't deviate from the plan unless it is absolutely necessary.

Once there was an anticipated use of force at a command where I was assigned that got out of control because an officer didn't stick to the plan. The inmate had been problematic and threatening to the officers most of the day. The area supervisor wanted to remove the inmate from the area before he attacked someone, however, the inmate refused to leave. So, the supervisor made the decision to forcibly remove him from the housing area.

The captain created a plan, similar to the one outlined above and entered the housing area with the extraction team. When these types of extractions take place the first thing the supervisor tries to do is reason with the inmate. The supervisor will attempt, one last time to get the inmate to allow the officers to escort him out of the area peacefully. While the supervisor is trying to reason with the inmate, the officers are positioning themselves so they can execute the plan if the supervisor cannot persuade the inmate to come quietly.

In this case, one of the officers was impatient and felt that the supervisor was wasting too much time talking to the inmate. He became frustrated and did not wait for the signal from the supervisor. He ran up to the inmate, grabbed him, and the two began to fight. The supervisor and other officers were taken by surprise. The plan was broken. They tried to salvage the plan, but it was too late. The cleverly planned extraction became a disorganized mess.

The inmate was fighting the officer that had initially grabbed him and the other officers were trying to subdue the inmate at the same time. The incident came to an end when the officers, supervisor, and inmate fell to the ground on top of the impatient officer. That officer's leg was broken in the fall. The incident was videotaped. In the video, you could see the officer's broken leg with his foot twisting in unnatural directions. His injuries were so severe that he never returned to the job and had to go on disability.

These types of injuries can be avoided if everyone sticks to the plan. Control your frustration and don't let your emotions get the best of you. I know that sometimes inmates may get on your nerves, but if you have a plan stick to it and give it time to work.

Key 32

Don't Rely On The Riot Squad To Save You

Work as if you only have yourself and the officers that are present to depend on if you have to fend off an attack.

I would like to begin by saying that during my career that spanned over nineteen years, I never saw or heard of a personal body alarm (PBA) malfunctioning during an emergency. For those of you who may not know, a PBA is a small box that has a red button on top and is worn on a correction officer's belt. The officer presses the button whenever he or she is being attacked or when immediate help is needed in an area, such as in a riot situation. When pressed, the button sounds an alarm in the jail's control room. A probe team or response team is immediately dispatched to that area while a riot squad is assembled to reinforce the probe team if necessary.

I have never seen the system fail. However, I am advising you not to rely on the response team *(the squad)*, to save you. The inmates know that if you press that PBA, the squad will be coming through the door in a matter of minutes. The officers know this as well, but what if something goes wrong? What if the squad responds to the wrong area?

What happens if there are several alarms going off at the same time? Will the squad be there in two, three, or ten minutes?

When you are working with inmates don't let the PBA give you a false sense of security. Work as if you only have yourself and your partners that are present to depend on if you have to fend off an attack. If you think like this, you will be ready if the PBA fails or some unseen mishap occurs that delays the response team.

Your life and well-being is your responsibility. Be prepared to defend yourself for however long it may take the response team to come to your aid. If that means that you should take a self-defense course on your days off, then I advise you to do so.

In many jails, officers are allowed to use chemical agents like pepper spray to defend themselves. It is incumbent on you to be proficient with the use of those agents. Pay attention when you are being trained in their use because it may save your life one day.

Take responsibility for your personal safety when working with inmates. Treat them the way you would want to be treated if you were an inmate. Don't abuse your authority. These are the ways to stay safe while working with inmates.

Key 33

Do not Underestimate the Insane

Those who have real mental problems do not think about the consequences of their actions before they act.

For many years, I worked with inmates that were under court-ordered psychiatric evaluation. The court will sometimes order that an inmate be evaluated to determine if he is fit to stand trial. Although I am not a mental health professional, I think it is worth mentioning that inmates that are under psychiatric observation should be closely monitored. You should have a heightened level of alertness when dealing with inmates that have mental health issues. Some of them are truly insane.

Those who have real mental problems do not think about the consequences of their actions before they act. They are very impulsive. I know you've heard that insane people have superhuman strength, and I'm here to tell you that in some cases this is true.

Never Underestimate an Inmate under Psychiatric Evaluation

The mental health professionals that evaluate inmates for the courts have reliable techniques to determine whether someone is truly unfit to stand trial. However, many inmates still think they can "beat the system" by trying to convince the psychiatrists that they are insane. It never works. The doctors are trained to know the difference between someone who is pretending and someone who truly has a mental health problem.

An inmate who feels this way will do almost anything out of fear and desperation. Inmates will still try to act out, so be alert and don't allow them to hurt you in an effort to convince the doctors that they are unfit to stand trial.

Some inmates who you will encounter will truly have mental health problems. Never underestimate those types of inmates, no matter how small or meek they may appear to be. They can go from being meek and mild one minute to being extremely violent the next. An inmate who had a mental health problem bit me, and I'm not sure he even knew that he had bitten me.

Do not taunt or make fun of inmates that have been identified as having mental health problems. Be professional. Be firm, fair, and consistent when dealing with them.

Their behavior is more stable when they have a routine. The problems usually arise when their routine is unexpectedly interrupted. They seem to have a harder time adjusting to new things than most inmates. So, once you have them accustomed to a set routine, try not to change it abruptly. If you must change their routine, be prepared for a possible irrational response. Stay alert, be cautious, and always keep inmates at arm's length. Do not allow inmates to invade your personal space, especially inmates with mental health problems.

KEY 34

IF YOUR FELLOW OFFICER IS ON DRUGS, TURN HIM IN

You are not betraying the officer; the officer betrayed himself.

If you know or suspect a correction officer is on drugs, the best thing that you can do for him, yourself, and your fellow officers is turn him in to the proper authorities. An officer on drugs is a danger to everyone. If your fellow officer is using drugs, his ability to think clearly is compromised. His ability to protect you is also compromised.

As officers, we often handle firearms, chemical agents, and other weapons that if mishandled can cause serious injury or death. Do you want the officer handling a firearm next to you to be high on drugs? I don't, and neither should you. You are not helping him by covering for him or making excuses for him. We all have problems, and we all get depressed from time to time, but drugs are not the answer.

If you want to turn your fellow officer in but do not want anyone to know that you did, you can make an anonymous call to the proper authorities and let them handle it. In New York City you would call the Inspector General's

Office. However, every jurisdiction has an internal affairs division. Don't be afraid to make the call. You are not betraying the officer; the officer betrayed himself and his oath to uphold the law when he chose to use drugs.

Although I highlight drug use, it could be any illegal activity. If your fellow officer is engaging in illegal activity, turn him in to the proper authorities. If an officer is doing something illegal, he may already be under investigation. If the investigation discovers that you knew the officer was engaged in illegal activity, but you did nothing, you, too, may become the subject of criminal and/or disciplinary charges.

Hold yourself and your fellow officers to a high standard. Do not engage in illegal activity. Do not accept drug use or any other illegal activity from your fellow officers.

KEY 35

KNOW WHEN TO STOP COVERING FOR A FELLOW OFFICER

Everyone must pull his or her own weight in order for the system to work.

Once, there was an officer named Peter Jenkins who would fall asleep on his post almost every night. His fellow officers always covered for him. They did his tours for him; they filled out his paperwork and woke him up every time the captain came to the area. C.O. Jenkins got so accustomed to his fellow officers covering for him that he would take off his shoes before going to sleep on post.

One night his fellow officers wanted to teach him a lesson. So, that night when Jenkins took off his shoes and fell asleep, his fellow officers took his shoes and hid them in the desk. Then they woke him up and told him that the chief of the department was in the building and on his way to their housing area to make a tour.

Jenkins jumped up and looked for his shoes. When he couldn't find them, he became frantic. He ran to each of his fellow officers asking if he had seen his shoes. With a straight face, each said he had not. Jenkins ran back and forth asking every inmate he saw if he had seen his shoes and each inmate told him no. One officer looked outside to into the corridor, then came back in and yelled, "The chief is coming this way!"

Jenkins was so worried that he looked like he was going to pass out. As he frantically looked for his shoes he kept saying, "How am I gonna explain to the chief that I don't have any shoes? I'll be suspended or fired for sure!"

After several minutes his fellow officers, realizing that Jenkins had learned his lesson, pulled his shoes out of the drawer and told him that the chief was not in the building. They had a good laugh at Jenkins's expense.

The point of the story is to emphasize that you should not make a habit of covering for your fellow officers. You may cover for an officer once in a while. But, if you make it a habit, the officer will eventually believe that he is entitled to this courtesy, and it will eventually ruin your working relationship with that officer.

Besides, constantly covering for someone else is not fair to you. Why should you do your work and someone else's when you are only being paid to do one job? Will the officer that you are covering for give you his check on payday? The answer is NO. Everyone must pull his or her own weight in order for the system to work. Don't let anyone take advantage of you. It is better for everyone if each person does his own job.

Once we had an officer in our command named Luis Calderon. Calderon would occasionally come to work drunk. When he was drunk, the other officers would cover for him. We would let him sleep in the locker room while we did his work for him. We would keep him away from the supervisors and the inmates. At first, he would only rarely come to work drunk. However, after a while, Calderon began regularly coming to work drunk. I guess, in part, because he knew we would cover for him. We all liked him very much because when he was sober, he was a terrific officer to work with. We thought we were helping him.

When the supervisors eventually found out that Calderon was coming to work drunk, they, too, began covering up for him, instead of suspending him like the rules require. Instead of helping him overcome his alcohol addiction, we allowed his addiction to worsen. We all became enablers. We weren't helping him, we were hurting him.

After a while, Calderon became very sick. Eventually, to our surprise, Calderon died as a result of his alcoholism. Calderon might be alive today if we would not have covered for him. He might have gotten the help that he needed. So, learn from our mistake and know when to stop covering for your fellow officers.

Key 36

Do Not Associate With Ex-Felons

Let go of friends and family members that are involved in illegal activities.

Many correction officers and prison guards (myself included) come from tough neighborhoods. I grew up living in public housing in Brooklyn, New York. Some of the friends I grew up with have been in jail and use drugs. When I became a correction officer I had to disassociate myself from them because they were involved in illegal activities. If you have friends or family that are ex-felons, or friends or relatives that engage in illegal activity, you must separate yourself from them. You don't have to disown them. You can still be their friend, but you must realize you are a correction officer. You cannot be involved in any illegal activity, and they should realize this as well. I found it best to keep contact with them to a minimum.

When I first became a correction officer, I went back to my old neighborhood and one of my childhood friends asked me to give him a ride to his friend's house. When we arrived outside of the house I asked him if he wanted me to wait for him. He then told me that he was going in to pick up some cocaine and that he didn't want me to wait for him because he knew I had become a correction officer. He said that he didn't want me to get into any trouble.

I drove away thankful that he told me not to wait for him. What if he hadn't told me he was buying drugs, and I had waited for him? What would have happened if he would have gotten back into my car with cocaine, and the police had pulled us over? I could have been arrested for drug possession or drug trafficking. I would have definitely lost my job. Thank goodness my friend was looking out for me, in a sense. I never put myself in that position again. I should have known better.

Sometimes you have to let go of friends and family who are engaged in those types of activities in order to grow and become who you want to become. As a correction officer, you have the opportunity to help yourself, your family, and your community. You cannot allow anyone to take that opportunity away from you. Correction history is riddled with stories of officers who lost their jobs because they just couldn't let go of their friends and family members that were involved in illegal activities. When you are off duty, stay clear of ex-felons and drugs users. Don't let anyone ruin your career.

KEY 37

STAY HEALTHY

Exercise is paramount to having a long, successful career in corrections.

There's one area where we can learn from the inmates. Most inmates realize the importance of daily exercise. They go to the gym or to the yard during their recreation hour and jog, play basketball, or lift weights. Many also have some sort of workout routine that takes place within their housing areas. They do push-ups, sit-ups, and pull-ups to stay in shape. Although we are not living under the same conditions that inmates are, we do work in the same environment. We should do some sort of daily exercise.

Many officers do maintain a daily workout routine. Many jails now have weight rooms and workout areas for the officers to utilize during their breaks and before and after their tours. But, too many officers do not maintain a workout routine. When we were in the academy as recruits, we all participated in daily physical training. Unfortunately, too many of us stop exercising once we graduated from the academy.

Jails are stressful places. Stress causes dis-ease, which can cause disease over time. The best way to counteract and relieve stress is with exercise. You may not be able to exercise as much as inmates do because working and maintaining a family does not allow you as much idle time as inmates have. But, you can and should carve out at least twenty minutes to one hour a day for exercise.

Daily exercise is paramount to having a long, successful career in corrections. I've seen too many officers graduate from the Academy then go on to gain twenty to thirty pounds in the span of a couple of years. Then, by the time they reach seven or eight years on the job, they develop high blood pressure, diabetes, or heart problems. If you exercise daily and eat right, you will be able to keep your weight down and avoid many health problems.

Smoking Cigarettes

Smoking cigarettes is a habit that officers should avoid. Most people, who were smokers before they became correction officers, increase the number of cigarettes they smoke daily once they become correction officers. They use cigarettes as a way to cope with the stress of working in a correctional facility. Smoking cigarettes is not the answer.

If you must smoke, do not smoke inside the jail. Most jails have poor ventilation, so the smoke just hangs in the air. Working in a closed environment like a jail increases the negative effects on your health. The secondhand smoke created by smoking in a jail also has detrimental effects on your fellow officers' health, as well.

So, if you are a smoker, I advise you to cut back on the amount you smoke or quit all together if you can. There are many smoking cessation products and programs available today like patches and gums, which were not available years ago. You should speak to your doctor about helping you quit or decrease your smoking habit.

Another thing you can do to stay healthy mentally, physically, and spiritually is take up a hobby. Some officers bowl, some take up photography, and some play a musical instrument or sing. A hobby is a good tool for relieving stress.

Key 38

Be Proficient With Your Firearm

You may find yourself in a life or death situation where you have to use your firearm.

Every correction officer should be proficient in the use of his firearm. I am not saying that every officer should or can be an expert sharpshooter. However, an officer should be able to hit the target that he is aiming at more often than not.

Although most officers will never have to use their firearms in combat during their careers, there is always that possibility. You may find yourself in a life-or-death situation where you have to use your firearm. It is best to be ready just in case.

Correction officers are responsible for supervising inmates within the jail or prison. We are also responsible for supervising them when they have to leave the jail or prison. When they go to court, the hospital, or when they are transferred from one facility to another.

Transporting inmates to and from these destinations also falls within our job description. Many escapes and escape attempts occur during the transportation of inmates. When an inmate is being transported outside the jail, there is a greater risk that the inmate may receive assistance to escape. Therefore, it is important that we know how to use our firearms correctly.

We also must be proficient in the use of our firearms just in case an inmate seeks to harm us when we are not at work. Inmates are released from jail all the time. An inmate may seek to do us or our families harm because of an incident that transpired in the jail. An inmate may want to seek revenge because he feels he was mistreated or treated unfairly while in jail. Remember, the inmates we work with are not angels and some of them are disturbed. So, you must be ready, willing, and able to protect yourself and your family at all times.

The instructors at the training academy's firing range can show you the proper stance, the way to hold your firearm, and the correct way to pull the trigger. But, they cannot do these things for you. You have to do them yourself, and you must learn how to do them well. The way you do that is by practicing. The only way you can become comfortable with your firearm is by using it. You must practice regularly.

Every jail or prison has at least one or two officers that are gun enthusiasts. These officers, if asked, will be more than happy to train you how to use your firearm. You just have to seek them out and ask them.

Or, you and a friend can join a firing range and practice together. That's what I did. A fellow officer and I went to a local firing range every week to practice our shooting. This really helped me become an excellent shot, and it made me more confident in my ability to defend others and myself with my firearm.

If you are carrying a firearm, but do not know how to use it, you maybe a danger to everyone around you. If you are ever in a combat situation where you have to pull and fire your firearm, you may not be able to hit your intended target. You may unintentionally shoot your partner or an innocent bystander instead. Or, you may lack the confidence to pull your firearm even though the situation demands you do so.

Some officers make the mistake of only firing their firearm when they have to requalify for the department, which is only once or twice a year. Firing your weapon once or twice a year is definitely not enough practice to be proficient with your firearm.

Some officers rationalize their lack of practice by saying that they always work inside the jail and never have to transport the inmates outside the jail, therefore, they don't have to practice using their firearm. This is a flawed argument because, as a correction officer, you can be called on at any time to transport an inmate to another facility, to the hospital, or to court. This is all part of your duties. You may have to transport a fellow officer to the hospital or have to defend your family outside the job. So, there is no reason you should not practice firing your firearm.

If you are having problems firing your weapon and do not have a friend or coworker to work with you, contact your training academy's firing range. The instructors will be eager to give you additional training because they know how important it is for you to be able to proficiently use your weapon.

Learning how to use your firearm is not just about

shooting, it is also about gun safety, which is just as important as shooting correctly. As you learn how to handle your weapon, you will learn how to safely load, unload, clean, and store your weapon as well.

Safety tips: Never pass anyone a loaded firearm and never place your finger on the trigger of a loaded firearm if you have no intention of firing it. Most accidental discharges happen that way. Place your finger on the trigger guard, which surrounds the trigger instead of placing your finger on the trigger. That's why it's there.

A pistol must always be secured properly in its holster to prevent an inmate or other individual from taking your pistol. Some officers do not properly holster their weapons. They fail to push their pistol all the way down into the holster because they are unsure of their ability to get the firearm out of its holster when it is pushed all the way down. If you practice putting the pistol in the holster and taking it out, you will become comfortable with removing it without hesitation.

It doesn't matter how big or small your hands are, you can become proficient with your firearm. If your hands are not strong enough to pull the trigger or to pull the firearm out of your holster, squeeze a rubber ball or use a spring-grip device to strengthen your hands.

With practice you can be proficient with your firearm. It is better to have the skills and not need them, than to need the skills and not have them. Prepare yourself now so you will be ready in the event that you have to use your firearm.

Key 39

Vacation

When your vacation comes around enjoy and reward yourself. You deserve it.

Can you see yourself cruising down the coastline of Bermuda on the deck of a catamaran or lying on a beach in Cancún, sipping on a piña colada? Or maybe you would rather ride a camel through the sands of Egypt, or take in the view from the top of the Eiffel Tower in Paris France?

Can you see yourself doing these things? I can see you doing these things because you deserve the best the world has to offer. You perform one of the most difficult jobs in the world. You work day after day with some of society's worst individuals, for this and other reasons you deserve to be rewarded.

When your vacation comes around, enjoy and reward yourself. You've earned it, and so has your family for supporting you each day. Be sure not to squander your vacation time by taking a vacation day here and there. If you must use a vacation day because you have a sick child or some other important reason, that's fine. But, do not squander your vacation days on unimportant things. Save enough vacation days to have a good and relaxing time when your vacation comes around.

It's always good to get away and forget about the job for a few days or weeks. Save your money and plan your vacation well. Your vacation time is time for you to do what makes you happy; it's a time for you to relieve stress and have fun. When your vacation is over, you should be well rested, recharged, and ready to focus once again on your job. Your vacation helps you cope with the stress that comes from working in a jail, so enjoy your vacation and have fun.

KEY 40

SPEAK RESPONSIBLY TO YOUNG OFFICERS

Young officers are looking to you for guidance. Your words carry a lot of weight.

Although all correction officers are adults, new correction officers lack experience when it comes to the ways of corrections. Sometimes experienced officers say things in jest that are taken seriously by the younger, newer officers. Young officers are looking to you for guidance. They are listening to what you say so they can better understand what being a correction officer is really about. Your words carry a lot of weight with new officers. The more time you have on the job, the more influence you have. For these reasons, you should never speak recklessly about using force or deadly physical force in front of new officers.

For example: If you jokingly say, "I would have shot that guy if he had pushed me like that" or "I would have slapped that inmate if he had said that to me," the newer officers may not know that you are just joking. A new, inexperienced officer may think that he or she must act that way in order to be a correction officer. This can cause problems for that new officer down the road.

If you are the senior officer, you have an obligation to act and speak responsibly. If you speak about using force, especially deadly physical force, take the time to be clear about under what circumstances force and deadly physical force can be used. Explain in detail what you are talking about and do not assume that the newer officers understand all the rules that apply to using force. Explain in detail what is permissible and what is not permissible. Teach the new officers that force should only be used as a last resort. When you speak responsibly, you are teaching the newer officers the correct way to view their duties, which will help them have a clear understanding of what it means to be correction officers.

Key 41

Rape

The area that you are assigned to is yours.
Know what's going on in your area.

Most people have never been to jail, but they have a mental image of jail being a place where rape is commonplace. A place where every other cell has an inmate named Bubba, whose sole purpose in life is to terrorize and rape his cellmate. Television would have you believe that jail is a place where gangs of sexual deviants freely roam the corridors and laundry rooms looking for potential victims. Where dropping the soap during a shower is always followed by a gang rape. This is not true. Inmates are always under some degree of supervision. Inmate rape is a real problem, but it is not as prevalent as Hollywood would have you believe.

Although officers cannot be in all places at all times, a good officer should have a general idea of what is going on with the inmates he is supervising. The area that you are assigned to is yours; it's like your house. You own it. If you know or suspect that an inmate is being forced to have sex against his will, it is your duty to take action to prevent the crime of rape from happening.

Most of the time, inmates who are being preyed on won't tell you because they don't want to be branded a snitch. So, you have to be intuitive and alert to the things that are going on around you. Sometimes, a look an inmate will give you will alert you to the fact that he is in distress. You must be aware of these nuances.

If you suspect that an inmate is being raped take some kind of action. Sometimes an inmate will talk to you if he is sure that the other inmates won't find out. So, when you have the opportunity to talk to an inmate that you suspect is having problems, out of earshot of the other inmates, ask him is anyone or anything bothering him? Sometimes he will open up and tell you what's going on. Sometimes he will seek you out and tell you things if he feels he can trust you. You have to create this type of environment for your inmates. You have to convince them by your deeds and actions that they can trust you and you won't expose them as being a snitch.

If you suspect that an inmate in your area is being harassed, try to talk discreetly with him. If he won't tell you anything then you may want to share your concerns with your supervisor. A captain or other supervisor can take the inmate out of the housing area and talk to him without the other inmates suspecting that he is informing. A captain can call the inmate out and say he is being taken to a visit, clinic, or commissary just to get him away from the other inmates.

Once they are alone the inmate can tell the captain exactly what's going on. A lot of riots, escapes, stabbings, and rapes are prevented this way.

Most inmates don't want problems. If they can make their stay in jail a little less stressful by telling someone in authority about things that are going on, they will—if they are certain that it won't get back to the other inmates. No inmate wants to be known as a snitch.

Being branded a snitch is one of the worst things that can happen to an inmate. Once branded a snitch, it is open season on him. Other inmates feel that they have the right to exact punishment on him. The inmate doesn't know who to trust or which way to turn. In cases where an inmate gives up very important information, it is not unusual for that inmate to be transferred to another facility or even have his sentence reduced in order to protect him and reward his deeds.

Unfortunately, some inmates who are in distress won't say a word to you or a captain no matter what, they will not tell. In this case you must still take action. If you strongly suspect that an inmate is in danger or being raped, move quickly to have him transferred to a safer environment.

Maybe it is as simple as having him transferred to a different housing area or maybe to a different jail. But, just don't sit there and do nothing. Most supervisors will work with you to prevent problems like this from continuing. A simple thing like transferring this type of inmate can prevent a death or other serious incident from occurring. It can also make life for that inmate better and your time at work go smoother.

Sometimes you will have a supervisor that you don't see eye to eye with. You may tell your supervisor that you think an inmate is in danger and needs to be transferred, and your supervisor may not agree. He may think that you're overreacting. In this case, make a note in your memo book indicating that you informed your supervisor of your concerns. This notation in your memo book is for your protection. If, at a later date, the inmate is seriously injured or killed, investigators will want to know what you knew and what you did to prevent the incident from happening. When you show them your memo book entry indicating that you told your supervisor about what you suspected was going on, you will be in the clear. Your supervisor will then have to explain why he didn't transfer the inmate or take some sort of action in light of the information you gave him.

If you feel strongly that your supervisor is not being proactive and a serious incident may result from his inaction, take the next step and make an entry in your post's logbook indicating your concerns. Most supervisors will read the logbook entries before they sign the logbook. Once the supervisor sees that you have made a logbook entry documenting your concerns, he may then take action. He won't be very happy about your logbook entry because you are in effect forcing him to take some sort of action. However, if an inmate's life is hanging in the balance, you can't worry about hurting your supervisor's feelings.

Some supervisors don't bother to read the logbook entries and just sign the book and leave. Supervisors should not do this because when they sign the logbook they are indicating that they have read the prior logbook entries that have been entered during their tour. In the event that something serious happens to the inmate, the investigators will go straight to the logbook and see your entry and then see the supervisor's signature and assume that the supervisor knew that there was a problem and took no action. He or she will be in big trouble and you will be in the clear.

Your goal should be to prevent an inmate from getting hurt and not to set up your supervisor, so let your supervisor know that you have made a log entry. Ask him to read it before signing the logbook. Explain that you are covering yourself just in case something happens. At that point, he may come to the realization that he should also cover himself by taking some sort of action. In any event, you have done your duty and now it is in your supervisor's hands.

KEY 42

OFFICERS HAVING SEX WITH INMATES

Inappropriate officer-inmate relationships are a breech of security.

Correction history is ripe with stories of sexual encounters between officers and inmates. It seems like every few years you hear a story about an officer getting caught having sex with an inmate. These types of relationships are frowned on by all correction departments and will always result in the termination of the officer involved. It can also result in criminal charges against the officer as well.

Inappropriate officer-inmate relationships are a breech of security. Officers who are involved in relationships with inmates lose the respect and integrity that an officer needs to be effective. An officer who will have sex with an inmate, will probably supply drugs, weapons, or other contraband to that inmate, or look the other way when the inmate violates the rules. An officer who puts himself or herself in this compromising position may even help an inmate escape.

Some years ago, a female officer became involved with a male inmate. When the inmate got out of jail, the officer got him to murder her husband. When the inmate was caught, he told how he developed a sexual relationship with the officer while he was in jail, and how she planned the murder. Now, they both are in jail serving time for murder.

Then there is the story of Officer Gleason who had an inappropriate relationship with a female inmate. Gleason aided her in an escape attempt by giving her a uniform and a fake correction officer's shield and identification card. Fortunately, when she tried to walk out of the jail, an alert officer recognized her and stopped her before she got out of the building.

The inmate told that Officer Gleason was waiting for her in a car on the other side of the Rikers Island Bridge. Gleason was arrested, and his employment with the Department of Correction was terminated, of course. You think that's shocking? Well wait to you hear the next story.

When I worked on Rikers Island at C-95, a male officer named Abrams was involved in a sexual relationship with a homosexual male inmate. Officer Abrams worked the midnight tour. He was bringing in drugs and alcohol to this inmate in return for sexual favors. It was revealed that the inmate became tired of performing oral sex on Abrams nightly, but he felt that no one in authority would believe him if he told on Abrams. So, that night when Officer Abrams demanded that the inmate give him oral sex, he bit Officer Abrams's penis and ripped a piece of his flesh off as proof that he was performing this sexual act. An ambulance was called to the jail and Abrams was rushed to the hospital. The inmate gave the investigators the piece of flesh he had bitten off Abrams's penis, along with blood for a DNA sample.

We were totally shocked because the Abrams we knew professed to be a devout Christian. He carried a Bible to work with him every night. He was also known to preach to the officers regularly in the locker room and the officers dining area. He was also married with children.

Jail is a strange place. The jail environment will corrupt your thinking if you allow it. It's a place where the vast majority of the residents are criminals, fallen men and women. The officers are always outnumbered. I've worked in housing areas where it was eighty-four inmates and only two officers—my partner and me. If you are not careful, being around inmates every day can turn your value system upside down.

Inmates will often try to persuade you to do the wrong thing. If they think that you are corruptible, they will pressure you to do favors for them. They will pressure you to bend the rules for them. Once they see you are open to persuasion, they will continue to pressure you to break the rules more and more. Before you know it, you've become just like them. You lose your moral compass.

Don't let this happen to you. Remember how you were raised. Remember all the time and money your parents and loved ones invested in you, molding you to be the responsible, trustworthy individual that you are. Don't let the inmates and the jail environment take that away from you.

Stay strong and be an example of correctness to the inmates. Let your deeds and action show them that you are beyond reproach and worthy of their respect and compliance. Maintain that strong sense of right and wrong that compelled you to take this job in the first place. Maintain your dignity and self-respect and let your light shine brighter than those who would try to lead you astray. Influence them to do what is right, instead of allowing them to influence you to do what is wrong. Remember who you are, and you will be fine.

Remember that misery loves company. The corrupt inmate loves to see an officer fall from grace.

KEY 43

THE SPREAD OF HIV/AIDS

Some inmates are HIV positive and suffer from different types of infectious diseases.

I have performed thousands of searches of inmates' clothing and property. During these searches I have founds drugs, alcohol, razors, shanks, shivs, knives, and bullets. However, the one thing I have never found is a condom. Unprotected sex is prevalent in jail. This is a problem because it leads to the spread of infectious viruses such as HIV/AIDS. Some of the men that are having unprotected sex with other men in jail also have wives and girlfriends on the outside that I suspect are unaware of their risky sexual behavior.

I've seen the toughest inmates in the housing areas hugged up with their gay lovers and an hour later I've seen these same inmates in the visit area with their wives, girlfriends, and children. Time after time, I saw women come to visit homosexual men, and it led me to wonder whether they knew or suspected the man they were visiting had a lover back in the housing area. I wonder whether this behavior could be contributing to the increase in HIV/AIDS and other infectious diseases in some segments of society.

In its infectious disease course, the Correction Academy teaches that one out of every four inmates is infected with the HIV/AIDS virus whether they know it or not. I have not been able to find any official data supporting this statement. However, I know from experience that many inmates are HIV positive and suffer from many different types of sexually transmitted diseases. One could draw the conclusion that a contributing factor to the increase in HIV/AIDS cases in America could be inmates contracting the HIV virus in jail and transmitting the virus to their unsuspecting mates when they are released from jail.

For this reason, I think it is a good idea to distribute condoms in the jails and encourage inmates to be tested for HIV/AIDS. It also would be extremely beneficial to educate the female visitors about the importance of being tested for HIV/AIDS and to have their husband or boyfriend tested upon their release from jail and before having unprotected sex.

Brochures with information about HIV and AIDS and the availability of health services should be distributed to the visitors when they come to visit the inmates. There should be a health care professional at the visitor intake area available to answer questions and start a dialog with the visitors concerning the transmission and prevention of HIV/AIDS.

Key 44

The Goldilocks Effect

When an officer neglects enforcing the rules they feel are "too hard" or "too soft".

The Goldilocks Effect occurs when officers enforce the rules they feel are ***just right*** and neglect enforcing the rules they feel are ***too hard*** or ***too soft.***

In the classic story, "Goldilocks and the Three Bears," the main character, Goldilocks, got lost in the forest and stumbled into the vacant home of the three bears. When she entered the home, she saw there were three bowls of porridge on the table, so she tasted all three bowls. One was too hot, and another too cold. After discarding the first two bowls, she ate the porridge that was in the third bowl that was just right. We all remember this story from our childhoods. Officers sometimes suffer from the Goldilocks Effect.

For example: An officer feels that the jail's policy allowing the inmates to watch television is too soft. He feels that our tax dollars shouldn't be used to purchase high definition televisions for murderers and rapists. So, in the morning when the inmates lock out of their cells, he doesn't turn the televisions on at 7:00 A.M. like the rules dictate. He turns them on at 10:00 A.M. instead of 7:00 A.M. And if a television breaks, this officer doesn't lift a finger to get it repaired or replaced. He leaves that for the officers on the next tour.

Another officer feels that the jail's policy concerning inmate searches is too hard. This officer feels that strip searching inmates is unnecessary because 90 percent of the time no weapons or drugs are found. He feels that inmates have enough problems and searching them only aggravates them unnecessarily. Therefore, when he has to search an inmate he does not do a thorough job. He only goes through the motions, and if his supervisor isn't watching him, he doesn't search the inmate at all.

In a jail, the rules are a product of years of experiences and trial and error. Most rules are a direct result of an incident or problem that existed in the past. A set of rules were put in place to solve that problem and prevent similar incidents from occurring. When we as officers begin to disregard enforcing certain rules that we decide are too hard or too soft, the security fabric of the jail begins to unravel. The following hypothetical example illustrates just how this practice creates a problem.

Prelude to a Stabbing

Three years ago, a brutal stabbing took place in one of the housing areas of your jail. After the incident, an investigation was conducted. It was uncovered during the investigation that the attacker used a metal shank to stab his victim. Earlier that day the perpetrator went to the law library where he got the shank from another inmate. He carried the shank in his pocket back to his housing area where he stabbed his victim.

The investigation determined that the shank would have been found if the inmate had been pat frisked before he entered the housing area. The stabbing would have been prevented. They also discovered that there was no rule requiring the housing area officers to pat frisk the inmates before allowing them to enter the housing areas.

In light of the information uncovered by the investigation, the warden implemented a new rule that instructed the housing area officers to pat frisk every inmate before allowing him to enter any housing area. He created this rule to prevent a similar stabbing incident from occurring in the future.

Three years ago, when the pat frisk rule was implemented, the stabbing was fresh in everyone's minds. Everyone clearly understood why this rule was created. Shortly after its implementation, the officers were pat frisking every inmate before entering the housing areas. Every officer complied with the rule, and the rule had its desired effect. In the months after the implementation of the pat-frisk rule, several dozen shanks were seized from inmates entering the housing areas.

Once the inmates realized they were being frisked every time they entered the housing area, they stopped trying to sneak shanks into the housing areas. The number of stabbings in the housing areas dropped dramatically. There were still slashings with small pieces of metal and razors blades because these types of weapons cannot always be discovered during a pat frisk.

Three years after the implementation of the pat-frisk rule, many of the officers that were working in the housing areas when the rule was implemented are no longer working in housing areas. Some of them work in other areas of the jail, while others have transferred to other jails. The vast majority of the officers working in the housing areas now were not working in the housing areas three years ago. They have never seen any serious stabbings occur in the housing areas and are unaware of the stabbing incident three years ago that led to the creation of the pat-frisk rule. They begin to question why they must pat frisk each and every inmate that entered their housing areas.

Some of these officers feel that the pat-frisk rule is too hard. They feel that it takes up too much time and causes more tension between the officers and the inmates. Some officers feel that the pat-frisk rule is unnecessary because they have never found a shank on an inmate trying to enter a housing area. As a result, many officers began to stop pat frisking the inmates entering their housing areas.

Three years ago, the supervisors emphasized the importance of enforcing the pat-frisk rule at roll call and reminded the officers of the brutal stabbing that had taken place.

Three years ago, when they toured the housing areas, they ensured that the housing area officers were pat frisking the inmates. Now, three years later, the supervisors rarely speak about pat frisking at role call. When they tour the housing areas, and see officers allowing inmates to enter without being frisked, they don't bother to instruct the officers to pat frisk the inmates.

The inmates notice that some officers pat frisk, while others do not. As a result, they begin to smuggle shanks into the housing areas once again. They also begin to protest when they are frisked now, which causes more officers to question whether they should be pat frisking the inmates.

Most of the housing area officers who remember the stabbing three years ago still pat frisk every inmate entering their housing areas, but these officers are few and far between. These officers are having more and more confrontations with the inmates that are resisting being searched. They are also having disagreements with the officers that do not pat frisk the inmates. Several months later, an inmate was stabbed to death with a large metal shank in one of the housing areas.

As we search for that elusive balance of what is "**just right**" we tend to lose sight of the big picture. It may be more convenient for you to ignore a rule, but you must ask yourself what are the potential consequences of my actions, or in this case, inactions? Do your actions make the jail safer or less safe? Before you decide to ignore or alter the effect of a rule, try to understand the purpose of the rule.

If after reading this chapter you realize that you are suffering from the Goldilocks Effect, rededicate yourself to performing your duties responsibly. Be sure to enforce the rules in the proper way, especially the rules that affect the security of the institution.

Life is full of opportunities, and corrections is just one of them. A career in corrections can be very fulfilling. It can give you the opportunity to have a happy and productive life.

And with that I will say good-bye for now. I hope you enjoyed this book as much as I enjoyed writing it. I hope this book helps you become all you can be. Remember, you and only you have the power to determine your destiny. Stay strong, and be well.

Sincerely,
Larone Koonce
Correction Officer, Retired

46510411R10139

Made in the USA
Middletown, DE
02 August 2017